S0-AED-553

Athina Onassis Roussel

THE RICHEST GIRL IN THE WORLD

The Onassis family legacy

BY THOMAS MARTIN

American Media, Inc.

ATHINA ONASSIS ROUSSEL
The richest girl in the world

Cover design: Carlos Plaza
Interior design: Debbie Browning

ISBN: 1-932270-12-4

First printing: September 2003

Printed in the United States of America

10 9 8 7 6 5 4 3 2 1

Chapter One

With the wind in her hair and the sun on her face the teenage Athina watches horses being put through their paces in the dressage stage of a Belgium grand prix equestrian event. Though young, happy, gregarious and full of life, Athina looks a picture of concentration and determination as she casts a critical eye on the cantering horses and their riders passing before her. This is Athina's dream world, taking part in the highly challenging sport of dressage, show-jumping and eventing. They have become the burning passion in the life of the world's wealthiest teenager.

Her love of horses is Athina's principal interest,

concern and inspiration. She lives for riding and horses, a hobby she took up as a young girl and pursued throughout her young teens. When she finally quit school at the age of 17, she took up competitive riding with a vengeance.

As her ability on horseback developed in her early teens, young Athina revealed the famous grit and determination inherited from her mother, Christina, and her maternal grandfather, famous shipping billionaire Aristotle Onassis.

Now 18 years old, Athina has also revealed that, like her mother, she had matured earlier than most young women her age. To many, the self-assured, attractive young woman with the long, flowing dark hair, perfect, unblemished pale olive Mediterranean skin and striking appearance looks older than her 18 years.

And, in company, Athina adopts the attitude and the conversational skills of someone far more mature than is usually to be found in a teenager. Athina is no airhead, no empty-headed, living-for-the-moment young woman who has suddenly discovered her freedom and wants to run wild, but rather someone who has already found herself and, importantly, a mission in life for which she is prepared to work with remarkable perseverance, dedication and single-mindedness.

Already she has an ambition in life: to represent Greece and win for herself a place on their equestrian team for the forthcoming 2004 Olympic Games to be held in Athens. That is a tall order, indeed an extraordinary ambition for an 18-year-old young woman who is not yet ranked in the upper echelon of Europe's best riders.

However, Athina not only has the iron will to achieve her objective but she also has the money to buy the very best horseflesh in the world. But Athina, of course, has an ace up her sleeve. In today's world of the big-spending, high-profile sport of equestrianism, the world's best eventers and show-jumpers can fetch in excess of $1 million. And in this league of big spenders, Athina has more cash to spend than anyone else in the sport.

In fact, give or take the odd million, Athina has some $1 *billion* she can call on. On top of that, when she reaches the age of 21, there will probably be *another* $1.5 billion in her name, invested in a myriad of businesses across the world.

Her father, Thierry Roussel, who had been married to her mother Christina Onassis for nearly five years, had tried to persuade her to go on to university, wherever she wanted, to complete her education, but Athina had other ideas. She felt that she had outgrown school, outgrown many of her school friends and had no wish to spend another three or four years furthering her education at a university. She felt ready to start a new life and to concentrate on what she really loved — riding horses.

As she told her father Thierry when he argued that she should attend university, "Why should I spend my time studying when I already know what I want to do with my life? You know I've set my heart on devoting my life to competitive riding and to do that at Olympic level means the more practice I get, the more hours I spend in the saddle, the more tuition I receive at the highest level, the better I will become. There are other people far better qualified and experienced than me to run the business."

And, of course, she was right. It may not have been the answer that her father wanted to hear but her reply proved to Thierry Roussel that young Athina had inherited the Onassis spirit and determination which had built one of the biggest fortunes the world has ever known.

It was in autumn 2002 that Athina, only 17 years old, decided that the Athens Olympics in the summer of 2004 was to be the bold target she would set for herself. It is difficult to underestimate the mountain Athina was attempting to climb if she was to win a place on the Greek equestrian team. Greece is well-known for the high caliber of its Olympic riders over the last few Olympics and Athina was starting at a level far below those fighting for places during the summer of 2002. Those six or eight riders expected to make their nation's Olympic equestrian teams are usually selected some two years before the games take place, but talented exceptions are sometimes included at a later date. Making her bid at the age of 17 was going to be a tough call and Athina's improvement had to be remarkable if not startling to make the grade. Of course, like all the others, she needs to be highly proficient in dressage, show-jumping and eventing and being excellent at one discipline and only mediocre or good at the other two will not win her a place on the four-man team.

There is no doubt that during the spring and summer of 2003 Athina made great strides in the sport but no one could tell her by August 2003 whether she was yet ready, or good enough, to take that giant step and be selected for one of the four places on the Greek team.

Already, in Greece, where Athina's equestrian career is of great importance with the Olympics approaching, she is known as *chrysomous*, "golden girl" in English, the same nickname that her mother had been given by her father Aristotle when she was born in 1950. Indeed, being the sole survivor of the Onassis dynasty, Athina is far more of a golden girl than her mother was as a teenager because she is already a billionaire. Now, some Greek sportsmen and women wonder whether it is just possible that this youngest child of an extraordinary dynasty might live up to her nickname and bring a gold Olympic medal back to the country of her ancestors.

If Athina's dedication, competitive spirit and iron will is anything to judge by, such a magnificent start to her adult life might just be within her reach. But it will take one hell of a lot of hard work on her part and on the part of those who will be coaching her in these three exacting equestrian disciplines to make that dream become a reality. There are those advising Athina who are suggesting that she should skip the Athens Olympics and target the 2008 Olympics, but she will hear none of it.

Athina has told some friends back home in Switzerland, "I just have this gut feeling that I will take part and that Greece will win a medal. It is, after all, the Olympic games and they are being held in Greece. Sometimes I wonder if my fate has been predestined and that I will help Greece win that gold medal. It would be fantastic, extraordinary if that happened but who knows. I have to go for it even if I don't make the team. I feel it in my bones and nothing will deter me from giving it a go."

Already she has taken one vital and important step in that direction. In the winter of 2002, Athina bought a great horse, a horse which experts suggest should be quite capable of taking part in the 2004 Athens Olympics. The gelding nicknamed Barber, a top-class jumper, apparently cost Athina around $ 1 million. And she was not the only Olympic hopeful bidding for the horse. For a rider to really become acquainted with a new mount and for others to judge the horse's real capability to make the Olympic grade takes approximately two years. As a consequence, those Olympic hopefuls searching for a great horse to carry their Athens Olympic challenge had to be purchased in the summer of 2002. And horsemen and women the world over were searching for those few elusive mounts still available. Like her grandfather before her, Athina showed that even though she was only 17, she had the determination to spend whatever was necessary to buy a great horse. From reports in the equestrian world, it appears Athina bought well.

Understandably, most of Athina's schooling takes place in private, far removed from prying eyes and certainly out of the reach of the most adventurous paparazzi. And, as ever, she is still guarded both day and night by a small team of armed SAS-trained guards, the elite British special forces division, who have surrounded her since the death of her mother.

Horse riding has always been Athina's passion and her favorite sport. As a child she always wanted her own pony and was given one when she was just 6 years old. Since then, Athina has owned some half-dozen ponies and since age 14 her mounts have been of a high class. But the man responsible for Athina's determination to attempt the Athens Olympics is a handsome Argentinian some 12 years older than she by the name of Alvaro

Alfonso de Miranda Neto, the son of a Sao Paulo businessman who won a bronze medal for Brazil in the Sydney Olympics as a member of their equestrian team.

It seems that Athina fell in love with the handsome Brazilian almost from the moment they met and in the summer of 2002 the two became lovers. That meeting changed Athina's life. She announced to her father Thierry and beloved stepmother Gaby that she had decided to move to Belgium to live with the man she had fallen in love with. And that meant she had made the decision to quit school, leave the family home in Switzerland and start to live a life of her own, mistress of her own life and her own future.

It was a bold and dramatic move for Athina to make. Young Athina has never led a normal life, simply because she is the richest young woman in the world. It is true that her father and stepmother tried to bring her up as an ordinary, though wealthy, Swiss young woman, but that proved impossible. She had to be protected.

Throughout her life there has always been a real and continuing possibility that some unscrupulous gang of criminals, or whatever, might try to kidnap her and hold her for ransom. And there are many occasions when such kidnappings end in the person's death, though often unintentional. The Roussels could never take any risks with Athina.

That was why since the death of her mother in 1988, when Athina was only 3 years old, her father and those Athens lawyers responsible for her and for safeguarding the Onassis fortune, decided to take dramatic steps to ensure her safety. Former British SAS troops were employed on a permanent basis to guard her home in Switzerland, which was turned into a mini-fortress with sophisticated electronic equipment to watch over every inch of the home and its gardens. The gardens are patrolled 24/7 by armed guards.

Whenever Athina had to leave the house to go to school, visit the local village, the dentist, her friends or go for a drive to the mountains, she would always be accompanied by an armed guard sitting in the front passenger seat beside a highly skilled driver. The vehicle would be armored to the highest degree with bulletproof windows and capable of withstanding a powerful high-explosive bomb placed in the road. Before each and every time Athina climbed into the vehicle, a check would be made to see whether a bomb had

been placed under the vehicle. When she
went out riding or visiting the stables she
would always be accompanied by those same
highly professional armed guards. When she
went skiing in the mountains they, too,
would accompany her.

When Athina went shopping with her
mother to buy toys, books or clothes or as a
teenager on her own when she wanted to
buy her own clothes she was always watched
over by the same armed guards. Of course,
they would try to be as discreet as possible,
carrying small, easily concealed automatic
handguns and Heckler & Kock machine pis-
tols, but they could never be far from her,
keeping a wary eye on any suspicious characters who might be around. Fortunately, in
the part of Switzerland, near Lake Geneva,
where Athina and her family lived there
were very few, if any, undesirable characters.
Everyone Athina met was kind and understanding and they realized to some degree
what life must be like for such a precious little girl who needed to be protected at all
times. But these highly professional men
were under strict orders to take no risks —
and they never did.

It was not surprising that as she grew older

and came to understand the extraordinary precautions being taken to protect her from any possible attack, Athina, firstly, came to understand that none of her school friends was treated in this way and, secondly, that she must be an extraordinary child to warrant such protection. From that moment, when she was about 7 years old, Athina knew she was different from any other child. And that has never changed.

Her parents and her guards tried to give Athina as much freedom as possible and they tried to treat her as a normal, ordinary child. But, understandably, that has proved impossible.

As she reached her teens and came to understand that she was the daughter of Christina Onassis and the granddaughter of the founder of the family's wealth, Aristotle Onassis, she learned over time that one day she would inherit this fabulous fortune. It would all be hers. Apparently, it took time for the young Athina to come to terms with the astronomic, phenomenal amount of U.S. dollars that she would be worth when she reached the age of 18. She was taken aback by the realization as her father explained that she would inherit the fortune because she was the last Onassis and her mother had left every single dime to the daughter she had so adored.

And suddenly, after Athina took her exams in the summer of 2002 at age 17, it appeared that she realized that she was now old enough to do exactly what she wanted, when she wanted. Though her parents had urged her to go to university she had realized that there was simply no need for her to attain degrees and expand her educational horizons.

She had met the Greek lawyers who, since her mother's death, have been responsible for investing and looking after her fortune. And she also had her father, who loved to advise her about everything in her life. Though her father took the responsibility to protect and care for his daughter with the help of $10 million a year from the Onassis fortune, it has been Athina's stepmother, the quiet, gentle, charming and down-to-earth Gaby to whom Athina has always felt close. To Gaby's everlasting credit she had always treated Athina as though she was one of her own children, giving her the same love, affection and attention as she has given her own three children — her son Erik, who is only 6 months younger than Athina, and daughters Sandrine, 16, and Johanna, 11.

Athina met the handsome Brazilian Alvaro in Belgium where she was training under the expert eye of Nelson Pessoa, the former world equestrian champion who runs an exclusive and highly professional riding school near Brussels, where many of the world's top riders are schooled and put through their paces. Pessoa is acknowledged in the world of eventing and show-jumping as one of the five best trainers in the world.

It was there that Athina first met Alvaro. She was smitten from the moment she set eyes on him. Here was the perfect man for Athina; handsome, witty, fun and very sexy as well as being a brilliant rider and a man who had represented his country — Brazil — at an Olympic games. Athina has reportedly told girlfriends, "As soon as I saw him, I knew he was for me. I was immediately attracted; he was like a magnet for me. He is just wonderful and I adore him."

Since last autumn they have been living together in a superb and expensive penthouse that Athina purchased at the top of an apartment block outside Brussels, the Belgium capital.

In her selection of lovers it seems that

Athina is following in her mother's footsteps because she, too, was always attracted to top-class horsemen and polo players. Christina, too, found them exciting and sexually stimulating men and great lovers and in her lifetime she enjoyed a number of them. She would happily talk about her polo players, describing them as attractive, aggressive, fit, well-built and prodigious lovers. Though still young and totally inexperienced, Athina would probably agree with her mother.

And, like her mother, it seems that Athina is also attracted to men with dubious backgrounds that most any mother would warn their daughter about.

Alvaro — nicknamed "Doda" — is tall, dark, slim, good-looking, mature and, rather importantly, formerly married with a daughter. However, the world of Olympic games and eventing does not make young men rich and Doda is no exception. He is reported to be financially poor and when Athina first met him at the stables, he was apparently having difficulty financing his lessons and keeping his beautiful then-wife Sibele Dorsa and their 3-year-old daughter in funds back in Brazil.

Once again, like mother, like daughter. Christina never cared about the past or current lives of her many lovers. She didn't mind if they were single, engaged, involved, married or divorced. She didn't care if they were rich or poverty-stricken. If Christina found herself attracted to them, physically and sexually, she would move in, sweeping aside any opposition to bed the man she desired.

Back home in Sao Paulo is Doda's ex-wife. The beautiful Sibele, formerly one of Brazil's top models, was not at all happy with her husband's decision to set up house with the world's richest teenager and feared that he's only attracted to her bank balance rather than the physical attraction of young Athina.

Sibele recalls that when her husband first met Athina he described her as "fat and fat." He also likened her to a baby elephant. Sibele explains that her former husband has always hated fat woman, making derogatory remarks about them and explaining that he could never "fancy" making love to a fat woman.

Perhaps that is one of the reasons why Athina has already taken drastic steps to reduce the size of her butt and her thighs, which she has surely inherited from her mother, who hated her own body. In a bid to please her lover, Athina visited Brazil in March 2003, shortly after her 18th birthday, and, reportedly, the clinic of Dr. Ricardo Lemos, considered by many women to be the world's foremost expert on reshaping ample derrieres by liposuction.

In Greece, however, there is fear that the young and inexperienced Athina might well be following in the dubious steps of her mother, buying her men. Throughout most of her life, Christina happily paid men to love her, marry her, divorce her or simply just have sex with her. Some have suggested that Athina's grandfather Aristotle "bought" the love of the famous Greek opera singer Maria Callas as some New Yorkers claimed that the principal reason Jackie Kennedy married Aristotle was because he had the wealth to protect her and care for her. Of course, from Ari's standpoint, he made no bones about the fact that he was buying the most famous widow in American political history, the former wife of assassinated U.S. President John F. Kennedy.

Her distant relatives also fear that their darling Athina has, by dint of genes, adopted her mother's approach to the opposite sex. They must have shaken their heads in disbelief that the beautiful, young, good-looking Athina should already be visiting doctors' offices for liposuction treatment when she already has so much to offer any man who is really interested in her. They worry that Athina might have inherited another maternal trait; enjoying being ordered about, even bullied, by a lover whom she adores. And, understandably, they want Athina to return to the bosom of her family, to her Greek origins so that they can care for her before she becomes too mature and too independent. Others fear that it is already too late. The die is cast.

They already wonder whether under Roussel's guidance and influence Athina has already been lost to Greece; that her inspiration and her schooling in Switzerland have given Athina more of a French-European outlook on life, the roots of her Greek forefathers already forgotten in the mists of time. Now they can only hope and pray that one day the golden girl of Greece will return to Skorpios and live among them.

Thus far, Athina has flown the family nest and she has not returned or even visited Greece. Instead, she has set up house with her lover, but she will shortly be faced with some of the most important decisions of her life. And they all relate to money.

She surely has no real idea of the family fortune; no real idea of the value of money and, so far in her young life, she has been spared the problems, the arguments and the legal battles that have surrounded the Onassis fortune ever since Christina died. In her short life, Christina showed a remarkable grasp of the innumerable complexities of the Onassis business empire and she grew the business during her short tenure at the top. But she did have a few years of learning the shipping trade in the offices of the Onassis empire in New York before her father died.

Throughout Athina's young life, legal battles have been waged without her knowledge between her father and the Athens-based Greek lawyers who were commissioned by Christina to take care of the business until her beloved Athina came of an age — when she could follow in her footsteps and actually run the empire.

Indeed, it was Athina's father who decided that he must have the right to bring up his daughter as he saw fit, despite Christina's uncle George Livanos having offered to raise the baby Athina as one of his family. The Greek trustees were only too happy that Athina should be brought up within a Greek family simply because she was Greek. George Livanos and his wife Lita have five children of their own as well as impeccable Greek connections. They also have homes in New York, London and St. Moritz.

As the arguments mounted as to whom should take care of Athina, professor Ioannis Georgakis, president of the public benefit Onassis Foundation, declared, "According to law, Thierry Roussel is the only and deciding factor in Athina's upbringing." He added, "I do not think that this child should undergo some of the bitter experiences that her mother had to endure with her unhappy family life."

However, during the early years of Athina's life, Roussel did give permission for her to visit the Livanos family from time to time but those visits became less frequent over time and, as a result, there has been little if no Greek influence in Athina's upbringing since her earliest years. Understandably, some of Athina's Greek relatives have described that as an abdication of Roussel's duty to his daughter because her mother and her family were proud of their Greek heritage.

Roussel's first decision was to move his family and Athina out of the grand Onassis home in Boislande, with its indoor swimming pool, where Christina had brought up Athina in her first years of life and where the young girl's earliest memories still lay. Instead, he built a $2 million ranch-style house 20 miles farther along the Route National 1 toward Lausanne on two acres of land just outside the village of Lussy-sur-Morges with a stunning view of the French Alps across Lac Leman.

Having set up the home's security system with the advice of professionals, hired nurses and nannies to care for Athina and, importantly, hired teams of professional former SAS guards to protect Athina, Roussel finally married Gaby.

Then the adventurous Thierry Roussel was off to seek his fortune. Always ambitious and certain of his own business acumen, Roussel had become obsessed with ecology and the environment, especially in relation to modern farming projects. Though he had never before been involved in farming, he claimed that by reading and research his ambitious plan would be a huge success. His plan was to make a fortune producing fresh vegetables out of season. On land he bought in Portugal, Roussel planted some 1,400 acres of strawberries, melons and tomatoes and on more ground planted 5 million trees. He claimed he was producing 100 tons of fruit and vegetables a day without the need of insecticides or pesticides. He toured Europe piloting his own private $2 million, eight-seater Cessna Citation, setting up distribution outlets across the continent.

However, in 1994, when Athina was 9, Roussel admitted that two of his farming projects had lost $15 million. Debt collectors even took his house in Portugal from him. His dream had become a nightmare.

Then he decided to build a private zoo in Portugal for the world's endangered species, but that came to nothing. He planned to write a book on how to save the planet. It came to naught.

Although married and with four children to bring up and care for, Thierry Roussel continued his amorous adventures, mainly with two young women, the tall, beautiful American model Teresa Prater and another stunning model, Kirsten Gille, who accompanied him on trips across Europe. Left behind to take care of the children was the lovely, long-suffering Gaby, the ever-faithful, adoring mother.

Later, Kirsten would relate one telling story, "As the excited Thierry, behaving like a young kid, showed me around the fields where he was cultivating strawberries, I noticed the earth looked dry. I asked him, 'Where's the water?' He replied, 'Oh, the water — I forgot the water.' "

To the intelligent Kirsten Gille, who knew Thierry really well over many years, that was the perfect example of Thierry Roussel and his great ideas.

Yet, shortly after Athina's 7th birthday, Roussel began a legal claim to Athina's fortune, demanding that everything should be turned over to him for safekeeping until she was 18. Understandably, directors of the Onassis Foundation rebutted this claim and called a press conference to tell the world of Roussel's claim. For all intents and purposes, the president of the business foundation, Stylianos Papadimitriou openly accused Roussel of trying to get his hands on Athina's fortune.

"Every year Monsieur Roussel receives money from the foundation for the care and protection of Athina. But he now claims the right to manage all of the Onassis assets, which we strongly dispute, and an issue that must be resolved in the Greek courts."

At that press conference, Papadimitriou claimed that Roussel was distancing his daughter from Greece and her origins. "Athina must be acquainted with her Greek roots," he said. "The child's fortune includes the private Onassis island of Skorpios, resting place of her mother Christina, her uncle Alexander and her grandfather Aristotle, yet she never visits."

In December 1994, the Greek trustees went to court in a bid to take control of Athina's annual allowance from her father. They sued in Switzerland, Greece and France over the right to administer her so-called "pocket money," some $1 million a year. The trustees claimed that Roussel was using that money for maintaining his property. That dispute would continue for a few years, but lawyers were convinced that the Greek trustees would never surrender the Onassis fortune to Roussel under any circumstances. And most believed Roussel had little or no chance of succeeding.

But all that changed dramatically when Athina turned 18 in January 2003. Now, she has meetings with the trustees, who explain to her exactly what she owns, what responsibilities she now must shoulder, what are the various and varied strands of the empire and what money she is now worth. It seems likely at present that Athina will be only too happy for the Greek trustees to continue their job of protecting the fortune while others who are employed by the foundation will continue their jobs running the various parts of the Onassis empire. And now any money that used to go to Roussel for his daughter's pocket money goes directly to her bank account instead.

The Greek golden girl, the wealthiest young woman in the entire world, has arrived on the international scene and thus far she wants nothing whatsoever to do with her wealth, her fortune or the Onassis empire. But the time is fast approaching when she will have to make tentative steps to understand her inheritance, although she might put off that decision for three more years, when she reaches age 21.

Chapter Two

Even before her birth at the American Hospital in Paris on Jan. 29, 1985, Athina was treated as someone extraordinary and very special. Throughout her pregnancy, Athina's mother Christina took every possible precaution to ensure that the baby she was carrying would arrive safe and well.

Christina was not in good physical condition when she discovered to her surprise and delight that she was pregnant. Within months of the death of her father in January 1975, Christina had been taking increasing doses of what was euphemistically called "medication." In fact she had become addicted to antidepressants and she discovered that the only way she could overcome her feeling of constant weariness and exhaustion was by taking increasing doses of amphetamines to give her enough energy to see her through the day. Christina was also taking barbiturates to help her get a sound night's sleep.

But over time, this nonstop daily round of drugs had taken its toll on her life, her health and her nervous system. To some of her close friends, Christina had become a shadow of the healthy woman she had been at the time of her father's death seven years before. But despite all the drugs she was taking, Christina was still fighting her prodigious weight problem — which not only seriously embarrassed her but also ruined her self-confidence and her ability to enjoy happy and full relationships with the men she fancied. To Christina, a good sex life was one of her top priorities.

Throughout those drug-taking years, Christina was grappling with the problems of learning about and running the multi-billion-dollar worldwide business empire that her father had bequeathed to her. Considering her personal drug problems, Christina showed that she was most certainly a chip-off-the-old-block because she seemed to have inherited her father's remarkable energy and ambition.

But, worse would follow as she wrestled with her drug problems and driving the business her father had built from nothing. Instead of attempting to kick the habit however, Christina resorted to taking shots providing herself with instant ups and downs. But because she couldn't face the prospect of injecting herself, she employed a full-time nurse whose sole duty was to administer the injections for her.

For the following three or four years, Christina took her nurse wherever she traveled across the world but, understandably, the more drugs she took the less their impact. And as time wore on, Christina was needing greater quantities to provide sufficient uppers and downers she needed to sustain her energy, calm her or provide her with a good night's sleep. For the two years before discovering she was pregnant, Christina had been on a downhill slope, unable to sleep at night and unable to keep alert during the day.

For a brief spell, Christina managed to survive without her daily injections after she met her second husband, Alexander Andreadis, the youngest son of another

Greek shipping millionaire family. Within a month of meeting, they were married; six months later, the marriage was over but only after a number of public and highly charged rows and violent arguments between the two.

One such storm occurred in the lobby of Monte Carlo's Hotel de Paris, when Christina decided to stay up until the early hours playing backgammon. Alexander stormed into the casino demanding Christina come to bed. She refused and continued playing. An hour later, Alexander returned to the casino, grabbed his wife and physically dragged her from the gaming table as Christina screamed abuse and lashed out at her furious husband. She sank to the floor and kicked at him while he struggled to get a grip on her. Her fellow gamblers looked on in embarrassment and shock, not knowing whether to intervene on her behalf or let the fight continue. Finally, after some minutes, Alexander managed to get an arm grip on Christina and he frog-marched her to the elevator and up to bed. Even as she was being marched toward the elevator she was screaming abuse and threatening dire consequences on her angry husband. She was not a happy lady.

Weeks later, however, Christina was telling close friends that she was pregnant and the baby, which she confirmed was a boy, would be named Alexander after his father. Two weeks later, Christina was denying the story that she had ever been pregnant. Those close to her were convinced that she had an abortion because she knew the marriage would not last. It didn't.

Christina's first marriage in 1971, at age 20, had been to Joseph Bolker, a man 29 years older than herself, ironically exactly the same age difference between them as between her own parents. Bolker was a twice-married, twice-divorced father with four daughters, a member of a wealthy American family involved in real estate. But his wealth wasn't in the same league as the Onassis fortune. In fact, Christina admitted later that she married Bolker on the rebound when still head-over-heels in love with the dashing Argentine polo player Luis Basualdo with whom she had enjoyed a romantic and passionate year-long affair. "Luis was the man who taught me all about making wonderful passionate love. He was fantastic," she would later confess, "but he broke my heart."

Bolker had no intention of re-marrying, but

under pressure from Christina's mother Tina and heavy emotional blackmail from Christina, Bolker eventually caved in. He came to the conclusion that he had little alternative but to go through with the marriage when Christina took an overdose of sleeping pills, nearly killing herself. Hours before Christina's dramatic suicide bid, Bolker had told her that he didn't want to get married to her or to anyone. He was perfectly happy as a single man with a large family to look after.

But Aristotle, her father, was more than upset at the news. In fact, according to some present at the time, he was angry and spitting blood when told the shocking news that, without a word to him, Christina had planned and married a man old enough to be her father, whom he had never met. In front of all those with him, Ari vowed to put an end to it. Wisely, Christina chose discretion rather than valor and stayed well away from her father, fearing his wrath. She wondered how he would react. She didn't have to wait long.

Having lambasted his daughter during numerous long transatlantic phone calls, Ari realized that Christina had no intention of ditching her husband, no matter what his views. But Ari had a plan. One way or another, he was determined to win this battle with his daughter whether she was in love with Bolker or not. At age 21, Christina was due to collect some $75 million from her trust fund. Ari sent her a simple message: "As long as you're married to that man you won't collect a nickel."

And he added an enticing rider, "The money is yours the day you divorce him."

But that wasn't all Ari had planned. He organized stories to appear in American newspapers suggesting that Joe Bolker had Mafia links and was not to be trusted. Other stories suggested Bolker's company was having financial problems. They were all lies, but the stories upset and angered both Christina and Joe.

And then, entirely by accident, Christina read a note sent from Ari to his son Alexander that she found in her brother's London apartment. The note left little doubt that Ari was planning to hire some heavies to beat up Joe Bolker, leaving him a broken and severely damaged man. That note frightened Christina and she immediately flew back to California, where she and Joe were living a happy, contented, married life. She would say later that their sex life wasn't the greatest but that Joe was kind and patient though she had soon discovered that he was no ball of fire. In bed, Christina liked her men passionate and highly sexed. But she knew in her heart that the note spelled the end of her marriage because she understood full well the lengths her megalomaniac father would go to end the marriage.

She arrived back in Los Angeles on her 21st birthday and to a surprise party Joe had organized for her. With tears streaming down her face, Christina told him everything and they agreed to part. They went on one last romantic holiday together, skiing in California's Sun Valley. Together they announced their pending divorce, Christina saying, "Although Joe will soon be my ex-husband, he will always be my best friend."

And then she phoned her father. It was the first time they had spoken since her marriage to Joe seven months earlier. Ari sent two heavies, armed with .45 revolvers, to California to escort his daughter back to Paris just in case anyone tried to stop her. Ari had missed his daughter but, of course, he was a very proud man and the proverbial wild horses would not have persuaded him to forgive and forget his daughter's so-called misdemeanor. Ari demanded total submission — and he would get it.

Ari was probably looking forward to the reunion with Christina more than she was. She agreed to fly to Paris in a couple of weeks, but first she wanted to take a few weeks holiday in sunny Buenos Aires so that she would be suntanned, healthy and in good shape to see her father. She also needed to get her mind in shape to cope with any challenges her father might throw at her after the long break in their relationship. She needed to re-invigorate her self-confidence. She hoped that Buenos Aires might be the place to raise her spirits.

Like her father, Christina was a highly sexed person who nearly always sought the sexual side of a relationship to give her confidence and because she wanted and needed the man in her life to find her sexually exciting and attractive. She needed to feel that men wanted her body, desired her sexually and found her physically attractive. To Christina this was very important because, understandably, she feared that every man she met, every man she fancied, every man she wanted a relationship with might only want her for her wealth. Worse still,

Christina had a life-long fear that men would want her not because of her wealth but simply because she was the daughter of one of the world's richest men. Such thoughts, which were ever-present with Christina, frightened her and, as a result, undermined her self-confidence.

But she did have the famous Onassis spirit. And she was convinced that a few weeks in Buenos Aires would give her back her zest for life. She decided to throw herself into her new-found single status by going on a shopping spree, treating herself to an entire new wardrobe. During her first 48 hours in Buenos Aires, Christina took a chauffeured limousine and was driven around the most fashionable parts of the city, stopping at every exclusive boutique and designer shop that struck her fancy. Back at her hotel suite she decided to rest and recuperate from her mad spending spree, which included massages and saunas, with people buzzing around her and attending to her every wish. Only then did she feel the confidence to launch herself into Rio de Janiero's famous annual wild carnival weekend.

Christina knew she needed a new man in her life and, more importantly, in her bed. As a result of curtailing her drug intake she now became worried about the other great bane of her life, putting on weight around her ample thighs and buttocks. Christina hoped that some serious partying and dancing might help get her into shape for a yet unidentified new lover.

She danced and partied with the famous Brazilian polo set nonstop and realized she had missed that invigorating lifestyle which always gave her a spark and renewed energy. Christina always felt intoxicated by the spirit and the high-pressure sexual excitement created by the famous Carnival. She spent 10 rip-roaring days and nights in Rio, her stay made wonderfully exciting and sexually satisfying after being introduced to a vigorous, compelling new lover, the handsome Brazilian polo celebrity, Paolo Fernando Marcondes-Ferraz.

Christina would say later, "I spent 10 days in Rio and most of the time I was in Paolo's arms or in his bed. It was wonderful and just what I needed. I left Rio feeling a new woman."

The 10-day break also made Christina realize that during the previous years she hadn't been enjoying herself sufficiently and so she decided to try and make her peace with the one man whom she had truly loved, the one man who had brought her real happiness, the Argentine polo player and legendary bounder Luis Basualdo.

Christina envisaged a return to their former days of passion and wild parties, sexual excitement and a devil-may-care lifestyle. She also needed Luis as her confidant, someone to whom she could tell all the details of the marriage, including all the sexual highlights as well as the problems of her husband. Christina had always poured out her heart to Luis and, for some extraordinary reason, she discovered that he was the one person to whom she could relate, usually in great detail, all the intimate details of her lovers and of their lovemaking. Luis had become her cathartic necessity, the one person who was happy to sort out Christina's emotional and romantic problems and with whom she could discuss all of the sexual peccadilloes of her lovers.

Christina threw herself at Luis. She told him that despite everything that happened to her, she was still in love with him and had always remained in love with him despite the other men in her life. But Luis noted that Christina had become a more independent woman since they had last been an item. In the past Luis had been the boss of their relationship, both in and out of bed. He made the decisions, told her what to do and what to wear. He ordered her about like no one had ever done before in her adult life and Christina discovered to her great surprise that she really enjoyed being the subservient partner to her enthralling, domineering lover. Luis could do anything with Christina, say anything to her and treat her with a certain disdain.

Christina would say later, "Luis was so masterful, I loved him for it. He was the first man to dominate me sexually and I was like putty in his hands. It started, of course, in the bedroom and the more he took control of me and my body, treating me like a rag doll, the more I loved and respected him."

At parties, Luis would hand Christina his empty wine glass to go and refill without a please or a thank you and Christina would dutifully obey, taking and refilling the glass and bringing it back to him while Luis carried on chatting to others. Of course, such a relationship between a polo player and the daughter of the wealthiest man in the world was duly noted and surprised all who knew her. Never in her life had Christina, a young woman always surrounded by maids and waiters, ever carried out such a menial task for herself or any man. But with Luis, she relished her role as the subservient mistress to her forceful lover and she wanted people to see and take note. Indeed, Christina would later confess that in the sanctity of their bedroom Luis treated her like a harlot and a slave, ordering her to carry out any sexual perversion he desired. And she would readily and happily obey, enthralled by every sexual antic he introduced to their love life and giving her the most fantastic orgasms of her young life.

But the Christina who had returned to Luis after her marriage breakup was a different, more independent woman. He soon discovered that Christina now had eyes for others, looking at other men, chatting to other men and flirting with them in his presence — something she had never done in the past. Previously, Christina had always stayed close to Luis at parties and whenever they were out together, she had eyes only for him. Their first weekend together after such a long break was once again full of intense love-making and passion and Christina believed that she was still passionately in love with Luis. But Luis knew in his heart that their moment had passed.

Within a week or so, Christina knew that she must leave Luis and keep the promise she had made to her father. But she now felt more self-confident, more capable of facing him. She flew to Paris for the reunion with her father only to discover that he was having grave problems with the two loves of his life — his wife of two years, Jackie Kennedy, the widow of President John F. Kennedy and Maria Callas, the famous Greek opera singer whom Ari adored and with whom he enjoyed an on-off love affair over many years.

Jackie had married Ari Onassis in October 1968, five years after the assassination of her husband and the marriage rocked the world of celebrities, socialites and politicians. Some newspapers echoed the sentiments of many. "Jackie, How Could You?" screamed one newspaper headline. It was the question half the world was asking. Jackie was a sophisticated, attractive, many would say beautiful woman of 37 with style, panache and charisma. She was at that time also the most famous woman in the world — the young, attractive widow of an assassinated U.S. president and the mother of two darling young children.

Onassis was then a 62-year-old, strong, well-built short man just 5-feet-5-inches tall, described at the time as "grizzled, with liver-colored skin, a fleshy nose and a wide, horsy grin." A former member of the Kennedy clan described the marriage as "ridiculous, preposterous, ludicrous, absurd, grotesque, rococo and positively stinks."

Jackie had first met Ari Onassis in 1959, when she was just 30. Jack and she had been invited to a cocktail party aboard Ari's famous yacht, the 325-foot *Christina,* moored off Monte Carlo in the Mediterranean. Also attending that party was Winston Churchill, then nearly 80 years of age. Jack Kennedy spent most of the time talking to Churchill while Ari showed Jackie around his fabulous floating palace. She was mightily impressed. The young Jackie had always been impressed with billionaires and Ari Onassis was the daddy of them all, a multibillionaire.

Following the death of her newborn son Patrick in 1963, Jackie accepted an invitation to take a cruise on the *Christina* with her sister Lee Radziwill and Franklin D. Roosevelt Jr. The cruise was a great success and a great tonic for Jackie, who was entranced by her enigmatic, enthusiastic, generous Greek billionaire host, who spoiled her rotten. She never forgot that cruise nor Ari's kindness and generosity when she needed cheering up.

Within hours of Jack Kennedy's assassination on Nov. 22, 1963, Ari Onassis flew to Washington, D.C., to express his condolences. Some days later, Ari invited her to a private dinner where he remained almost silent as Jackie's tears flowed down her cheeks as the shocked, grief-stricken young widow poured out her heart. At one point, Ari held her close as she sobbed into his shoulder.

Over the next few months, Onassis began to quietly and surreptitiously court Jackie, inviting her to private dinners, the ballet and the opera. As Jackie came to terms with her husband's murder, Onassis became more relaxed, taking her to small Greek restaurants in New York where he danced traditional male-only Greek dances and broke dishes on the floor in true Greek style. In 1968, Jackie accepted another invitation to cruise on the *Christina* in the Caribbean and Onassis popped the question. It is understood that at this time Ari Onassis had never made a pass at Jackie, kissing her only on the cheek when greeting her and saying goodbye. They had never embraced passionately or made love.

Jackie wanted to say "yes" immediately because she had come to realize that Ari could offer a life of wealth, privilege and, more importantly, privacy. But there were too many imponderables to consider before giving Ari an answer. She worried mostly how Caroline and John would take Ari as their new father figure; how the Kennedy family would accept Onassis; how the Catholic church would react to her marrying a member of the Greek Orthodox church; how the American people would react, and whether marrying Onassis would rob her brother-in-law Robert Kennedy of winning the Democratic nomination for president.

It must be remembered that Jackie owed Bobby Kennedy the most extraordinary debt of gratitude. It was Bobby who came to her rescue after Jack's assassination. Jackie would say later, "Bobby saved my sanity. I was in the most desolate state, unable to control my feelings or my mind. One moment I would be smiling, the next I would be in floods of tears, unable to control my emotions. Bobby saved me and made me realize I had to continue for the sake of Caroline and John. He made me realize that they needed me to get through their trauma."

The murder of Bobby Kennedy on June 4, 1968, when he was on the verge of winning the Democratic nomination for president, plunged Jackie into a new and even greater emotional crisis than she had experienced following Jack's murder. Now she really felt that she was going insane. Bobby's murder had taken away the most important person in Jackie's life. He had become her emotional crutch, indispensable to her precarious morale and now he, too, had been taken from her in yet another moment of madness that seemed to plague the Kennedy clan.

For a time Jackie did, indeed, lose her mind. The shooting of Bobby became mixed up in her mind with the killing of her husband five years earlier. Friends and Kennedy family members found Jackie carrying on conversations as though Jack was still alive, relating events they were to attend in the future and discussing the family with him. But she would be talking to no one, sometimes in a room on her own and, understandably, that worried her doctors and those who knew her well.

Ari Onassis was in Greece when the shooting of Bobby occurred and he immediately flew in one of his private jets to Los Angeles. Ari would say later, "I found Jackie in a state of panic and disbelief, occasionally lapsing into dialogue that indicated she was confusing both assassinations."

To his credit, Onassis never left her side. He flew her to New York and was at her side during the funeral service in St. Patrick's Cathedral. Indeed, it was the horrendous impact of Bobby's murder coming so soon after Jack's assassination that convinced Jackie that she needed someone to care for her and to take all her troubles away. Ari fitted the bill in more than one way.

Jackie said later that it was never Ari's money that persuaded her to marry him. There were two reasons: emotional security for herself and, more importantly, physical safety for her beloved children. It was true that Jackie was not a wealthy woman — she had only the income from a $200,000 trust fund to live on. But it was not the money that persuaded her. At that time in 1969, Jackie lived in fear of someone or, perhaps, some organization with a grudge against the Kennedys, who might want to kill her or Caroline or young John. Ari's money could protect them all.

And so it proved.

But the relationship between Christina, in particular, and Jackie was fraught with jealousy and problems from the beginning. When Jackie married Ari in October 1968

Christina was an 18-year-old teen, whom her father affectionately called *chrysomous* — Greek for golden girl. At that time Christina thought her father only had eyes for her, that she meant everything to the father she adored and with whom she believed she had a special relationship since her parents divorced in 1960. At the time of her parents' divorce, Christina was an impressionable 10 years old, enthralled by her famous father. Her brother Alexander also strongly objected to the marriage because he feared the Onassis fortune would be bequeathed to Jackie and her children rather than to him and his sister.

At 18, Christina had everything a girl could wish for, including a magnificent penthouse in Paris, a majestic villa in Glyfada, an exclusive and fashionable Athens suburb, and an allowance she couldn't spend. But Christina missed her father, whom she rarely saw and who had so little time for her. Indeed, Christina had grown up rarely seeing her father on a regular basis because he spent so much of his time flying around the world checking his shipping interests, attending high-level business meetings and holding discussions with senior officials of a number of governments. Ari loved his hectic, nonstop life; Christina hated it.

The awkward, passionate Alexander, whom some described as the quintessential angry young man, confronted his father time and again from the moment he heard that he was to marry Jackie Kennedy. Aides recalled fierce shouting matches between Ari and Alexander as Ari tried to persuade his son that he and Jackie Kennedy both needed each other and that he was being a kind, considerate and generous man in marrying Jackie, who needed someone to care for and protect her. Alexander would tell his father that he only wanted to marry Jackie so that he could show off to the world the prize his wealth had bought him.

Famously, Alexander was heard screaming at his father, "You've bought Jackie Kennedy as though she was some slave put up for sale in some market in ancient Greece. It's despicable. This whole marriage stinks."

Ari was furious at such attacks from the son whom he had always spoiled and adored, but Alexander would not be so insulting when talking to the media. In public, Alexander would only say, "I didn't need a stepmother but my father needed a wife."

However, Ari's marriage to Jackie did

bring together Alexander and Christina as they sought ways to prevent the wedding from taking place. But even their combined opposition could not stop their determined father from marrying the world's most celebrated and famous widow.

But though Christina came to accept her stepmother, Alexander never did so. He always feared that the world's most celebrated and much-loved widow had only married his father to gain his wealth for her own children. Alexander read the newspapers. He knew that Jackie was not wealthy and he also knew that she liked the very best things in life. Not for a moment did Alexander ever believe his father's marriage was a love-match. Until the day of his untimely and tragic death in a plane crash at age 25, Alexander convinced himself that Jackie had married his father solely for money and that, in reality, his father had simply bought Jackie for the price of one of his aircraft. They had both got what they wanted.

On one famous occasion, Alexander turned to his stepmother and spoke in a loud voice at one of his father's parties on his island of Skorpios that was attended by 100 celebrities and socialites from New York, London, Paris and Athens, "You don't think marrying for money is so bad, do you?"

Those near enough to hear the remark, which required no reply, were stunned that Alexander should make such a comment that was so obviously intended to embarrass Jackie in front of her guests. For her part, Jackie refused to be drawn. She gave Alexander one filthy look, turned her back and began chatting to guests. Alexander stormed off.

In part, Alexander was right. Now that the facts of that marriage have been ascertained, it is accepted that Ari Onassis paid Jackie $3 million at the time of their wedding and he set up a $1 million trust fund for Caroline and John to be paid while they were still minors, and that if Jackie and Ari were divorced he would pay her an annual sum of $100,000 for the rest of her life.

From Jackie's point of view that was a great deal; from Ari's viewpoint it was a small price to pay for the world's most celebrated and beautiful young widow of a famous American president.

Jackie understood, however, that many of her friends, many of Jack Kennedy's family and friends were unhappy at her marriage to Ari

Onassis because, whether they spoke openly or kept a discreet silence, most of them felt that the marriage must have been based on money. One Kennedy insider said at the time, "Why on earth would Jackie think for one moment of marrying such a fat, ugly, little man like Ari Onassis unless it was for his money." And he even provided the answer, saying, "She wouldn't, would she?" It was a rhetorical question.

Indeed, Jackie was convinced that no one ever believed that she had married Ari for any reason except to provide her with the protection from the media that she needed and the lifestyle for which she had craved since her teenage years. It is undeniable that Jackie loved the high life and she adored being the wife of the president of the United States.

To her very few close friends, however, Jackie would say, "None of you realize how kind and generous Ari has been to me. He is the kindest, most considerate man I've ever met. He's also warm. He has a sense of humor that makes me laugh and when I am with him I feel not only happy but secure. And that's really important to me."

But there were few who wanted to hear such sentiments from the widow of one of America's most loved presidents. At the time of his death,

Jack Kennedy had won over many Republicans, primarily due to his successful handling of the Cuban missile crisis. He had also won tremendous affection and praise from most Democrats. Perhaps more importantly Jack Kennedy had won the hearts and minds of not only the great majority of America's young people but also millions of young people around the world who looked to him for leadership and inspiration. He provided that in buckets and they came to respect him for providing such leadership. After his assassination, young Americans and many young people throughout the Western world came to honor and revere him, some to almost love him.

In 1972, Jackie broke her unwritten rule and spoke candidly to a journalist about the changes in her life and in herself in the four years since her marriage to Ari.

She told the Iranian reporter Maryam Kharazmi of the English-language newspaper *Kayham International*:

> *Why do people always try to see me through the different names I have had at different times? People often forget that I was Jacqueline Bouvier before being Mrs. Kennedy or Mrs. Onassis.*

Throughout my life I have always tried to remain true to myself. This I will continue to do as long as I live.

I am a woman above everything else. I love children and I think seeing one's children grow up is the most delightful thing any woman can think about.

I have been through a lot and I have suffered a great deal, as you know. But I have had lots of happy moments as well.

I have come to the conclusion that we must not expect too much from life. We must give to life as much as we receive from it.

Every moment one lives is different from the other, the good, the bad, the hardship, the joy, the tragedy, love and happiness are all interwoven into one single indescribable whole that is called life.

The truth of the matter is that I am a very shy person. People take my diffidence for arrogance and my withdrawal from publicity as a sign, supposedly, that I am looking down on the rest of mankind.

After their marriage, Christina noted how her father dealt very differently with Jackie's two children Caroline, who was 11 at the time of her mother's wedding to Ari, and John, who was just 9. It seemed that Caroline, who had loved and adored her father, found her mother's second marriage very difficult to accept. She found it almost impossible to come to terms with the fact that her mother could possibly have fallen in love with a man like Ari Onassis, who was Greek, fat, old and ugly when her own father was young, handsome and world-famous. The marriage just didn't make sense to Caroline and she simply didn't like her mother taking such a dramatic step so soon after her father's death.

But 9-year-old John was different. Ari found it far easier communicating with John, telling him that they would become buddies and they did. Ari went out of his way to ensure there was a good relationship between the two of them. Ari would spend hours taking John sailing, fishing and waterskiing. Indeed, Ari seemed determined to become the model parent to John and gave him far more time than he had ever given Alexander, his own flesh and blood. Ari taught John some Greek and the two developed a remarkable relationship, spending time together on Skorpios when John was on vacation from school. Indeed, it is true to say that the two came to really like each other. Her son's close relationship with Ari gave Jackie confidence that she had made the right decision in marrying him.

Teenage Christina, however, was fascinated that Jackie Kennedy would ever contemplate marrying her father, let alone going through with the idea. She wondered why on earth Jackie would marry him and, like her brother, she not only feared but was absolutely certain that Jackie had only married him for his money.

But she had much greater confidence in her father than Alexander ever had. In essence, Christina trusted her father not to hand over the family silver, along with his shipping lines, his fleet of aircraft and his millions of dollars to a woman he hardly knew. Christina still had faith that her father loved her, his only daughter, and would always do so. As a result she came to accept the marriage and hoped that her father would be happy married to such a glamorous and famous woman. Secretly, she had her doubts but she kept those to herself.

Christina would watch the marriage closely, search for any signs of problems, spats,

about the mother she never knew and had always yearned for. For as long as she could remember, Athina had grown up being cared for by her surrogate mother, "*Papa's*" wife, the beautiful Swedish model Marianna "Gaby" Landhage.

It was only a few years ago that Athina discovered, surely to her shock and surprise, that her own father had fathered two children with Gaby while married to her mother Christina. It was in March 1984 that Christina and Thierry Roussel married at a glittering wedding ceremony in Paris and 10 months later Athina was a born, a healthy 6-pound, 2-ounce baby.

Athina read that only a few months later, Christina learned that her husband of less than a year was once again having an affair with his former girlfriend Gaby Landhage. And, to Christina's consternation, Gaby was about to have Thierry's baby. To Christina, the arrival of her beautiful Athina was the greatest moment of her hectic life and she had been so happy the handsome Frenchman Thierry Roussel was Athina's father. Christina believed that fathering Athina had also been of the greatest importance to Thierry because now they were a real family unit.

Six months after Athina's arrival, Gaby gave

birth to Thierry's son Erik in Malmo, Sweden. And as Athina read, she must have understood and sympathized with her mother's understandable shock, humiliation, anger and disappointment at her faithless husband's adultery.

Christina would say, "I can understand a man being unfaithful at some time in his life, but we were so happy together. Gaby was no new lover because she had been his on-off mistress for 10 years. I just feel so totally devastated. How could he?"

The innocent, deep-thinking teenage Athina must have felt the same way as her mother had all those years ago and, as a result, she probably now looked differently on the man who had brought her up, loved and cherished her, shared the highs and lows of her young life, and had always seemed so proud to be her father.

That realization, that one simple fact, surely changed the way Athina thought of her father, whom until that moment she had loved and respected above any other man. No more. And though still a young teenager, Athina probably wondered if her relationship with her father would be repaired, could be repaired, or whether this was the moment that she became an adult who now had to think for herself.

Athina read more and learned more.

She read that within a matter of months, Christina had forgiven her husband for his misdemeanors, invited him to visit her at her home in Switzerland and within days he was sharing her bed once again. They became a couple and it seemed their marriage was back on track. But it would not be for long. It soon became obvious to Christina that Thierry was again seeing Gaby and, in June 1987 Gaby gave birth to another of Thierry's children, a daughter they named Sandrine Helene Francine.

This time Christina could take no more and she ordered an immediate divorce. At about that time Christina also let it be known to friends and relations that during the few years of their marriage she had given some $57 million to Thierry. Her relations, in particular, were taken aback by her remarkable generosity, while others considered her generosity foolish in the extreme.

Reading such matters, Athina must have been somewhat surprised to discover that sometime later her mother had decided to make friends with her great rival, inviting the beautiful Gaby, her son Erik and baby Sandrine to her 18-room villa, La Boislande,

in the Swiss village of Gingins, 12 miles outside of Geneva. La Boislande was to become
the only residence Christina ever called home.
A staff of 10 was employed on a permanent
basis to keep the place aired and ready for the
arrival of Christina "at any moment."

Apparently, the meeting between the two
women went really well, primarily because
Athina and Erik played happily together
while baby Sandrine lay gurgling in her cot.
That meeting had a deep effect on Christina
because she suddenly came to the conclusion
that she, too, wanted another baby. And, once
again, she wanted Thierry Roussel to be the
father. During the next few months, Christina
took every opportunity to have sex with
Thierry in the hope that her dream would
become a reality. She bought him whatever he
wanted, indulged him hopelessly, carried out
his every whim and wish and twice she
became pregnant. But on both occasions a
miscarriage followed in a matter of weeks.

Athina read of her mother's awful plight. She
also read that she found it difficult to carry a
pregnancy to term because of the drugs and
the alcohol she had taken during her life and
the savage dieting she had occasionally prac-
ticed. It seemed the idea of another baby

became an obsession for Christina and, as a result, after the second miscarriage, an unhappy and highly emotional Christina went into a deep depression.

Christina may have been down but she had the guts to pull herself together. Successfully kicking the depression, Christina planned an extraordinary holiday in the summer of 1987, a vacation which mystified all those who knew that Thierry was serving both his mistress Christina and his wife Gaby. Christina rented the splendid villa Le Trianon in St. Jean-Cap Ferrat on the French Mediterranean coast for the months of July and August for Athina and herself and her lover Thierry. She also rented the villa next to hers for Gaby and her two children so that her occasional lover Thierry would not need to be too far away from Christina in case his services were needed. Apparently, though the setup was unusual, it seemed to work very well with Christina, Gaby and the three children spending many days together.

As Athina came to discover later, her mother enjoyed owning and collecting properties for herself like some men collected cars. At that time she not only owned and frequently stayed at La Boislande, but also owned Villa Crystal in St. Moritz, which she bought in 1976; a fabulous duplex on the Avenue Foch in Paris, with an entire floor reserved for entertaining, that she bought in 1984; an apartment in London's Eaton Square, and, of course, the famous Onassis private family island Skorpios off the Greek coast where a staff of 40 was permanently employed. This wild, 500-acre uninhabited scrub and rock in the Aegean had been her father's pride and joy. He had spent a fortune converting the island into a wonderful, luxurious, private holiday island with a few lovely villas for friends and relations and a deep-sea port for his spectacular yacht *Christina*.

Before Athina learned of her father's adultery with her stepmom she had probably, naturally, asked him a hundred or more questions about what her mother was like; whether she was beautiful; whether she was kind and loving; whether they were happy together. And when very young, Athina asked her father whether her mother had loved her.

Of course, her father must have tried to answer every question she threw at him in a positive way because he had no wish to portray Christina in anything but a good light. Thierry wanted his daughter to know the truth, that her mother was loving and caring, engaging and attractive and someone who cared for her above all else.

As Athina grew from childhood to puberty she became increasingly aware that she was no ordinary child of a well-off, suburban middle-class Swiss family. It appears that as if by instinct, Athina felt there was something special about the Onassis name and she always used her full name, Athina Onassis Roussel. She came to realize that the mothers of her friends at school treated her in a special way, making a fuss of her, frequently inviting her to their house to play, and she came to recognize that her name was different from every other girl in the Swiss school she attended. It was obvious that her looks were somewhat different from virtually every other girl at the school as well. Athina was darker, her skin a beautiful olive color, her eyes darker and her entire appearance more striking than the other girls. And, as with her mother, Athina, too, reached puberty at an early age, a couple of years before the other girls in her class.

And since she had barely known her mother, Athina was inquisitive to read all she could about her, trying to understand what had happened in her life to bring it to such an early end. She probably read with fear and apprehension of what she might find, primarily because her father, for whatever reason, did not appear to want his daughter to dig into the family past, discovering facts and asking questions.

He knew that the teenage Athina might mistake fiction for fact, construe happenings and occasions inaccurately, unable to comprehend the haphazard and complicated relationship between him and her mother Christina. Their relationship had been far, far different from any that the teenage Athina had ever come across. She was still far too young to understand everything that had happened in her mother's life and in the Onassis family and, understandably, Thierry wanted to shield his darling daughter from facts that might upset her.

He fully intended to tell his daughter everything when she was of an age to comprehend such matters. But he didn't want her to become distressed or upset by reading or hearing of rumors and stories that were only half-truths. All he had yet to decide was at what age he would do so. He came to the conclusion that perhaps after Athina's 18th birthday he would readily answer any questions she cared to ask him about the Onassis family and the ramifications of relationships and affairs that for decades had been the stuff of newspaper articles and gossip, truthfully and honestly.

Understandably, Thierry feared that Athina might come to the conclusion that he was partly responsible for her mother's early death because their relationship had fallen apart just before. And that, of course, was the last thing he wanted her to believe.

But after her 15th birthday Athina apparently wanted to discover for herself what she perceived were the secrets of the Onassis family. So she began by reading books about the Onassis family history; of the many marriages but, more specifically, about the marriage that had captured the attention of the world, the marriage of her grandfather Aristotle Onassis to the widow of the famous U.S. President John F. Kennedy.

Athina was must have been upset for the mother she never knew when she read that her grandfather Ari and his first wife Tina had not even wanted Christina. Her conception had been an accident. Two years earlier, Ari's teenage wife Tina had given birth to their son Alexander and then on two other occasions when she became pregnant she had agreed to have an abortion. The only reason Tina, just 21 at the time, did not have an abortion with Christina was a warning by the doctor that it could endanger her health and prevent any more pregnancies at a later date. Christina arrived in the world unwanted and unloved. It made Athina sad just reading about it.

Neither Alexander nor Christina had happy childhoods. It seemed that neither Ari nor Tina cared too much for parenting, leaving their children alone for months at a time in the care of nannies or relatives while they spent their lives flying around the world. Indeed, to many it seemed that Tina actually nursed a secret hatred for her daughter, whom it seemed she was ashamed to have produced because Christina was no beautiful child. She was very dark, with big, dark eyes and huge black circles beneath them as though she had been crying for days on end. Her mother thought her ugly.

Christina recalled that she never really enjoyed a childhood, looked after by nannies, educated by tutors, eating with servants, traveling with bodyguards and leading a lonely, unloved life. All the young Christina yearned for was her father to love her. But he didn't.

Athina realized that the mother she never knew would have been only a few years older than she was, some 18 years of age, when Ari married Jackie Kennedy in 1968. That fascinated Athina because she had seen the photographs of the two together and she must have wondered in her youth and her innocence how the lovely Jackie could have fallen in love with such a man. And she probably wondered what her own mother had thought of the marriage.

Her reading revealed that her mother watched her father's marriage rather closely because she never totally trusted Jackie Kennedy's motives in marrying her father. And Athina would also read how her mother became fascinated by her father's marriage to the most beautiful and famous widow of her time.

The books revealed that despite all the pessimists, the first two or three years of their marriage were indeed happy. Jackie had needed the emotional and physical security that Ari Onassis and his money provided in abundance, as well as the stability and emotional security she yearned for ever since her world was shot to pieces with Jack's horrendous killing.

Athina also read books about President Kennedy's assassination and the man theories and reasons behind it. And she wanted to try to understand Jack Kennedy, the president, the husband, the father so that she could understand how the Kennedy clan became entangled with the Onassis family. Athina wanted to know and understand how the assassination had affected Jackie and why she had married her grandfather.

Athina read that ever since that morning in Dallas in November 1963, Jackie had failed to come to terms with that famous car ride from the moment the fatal shot hit her husband, when she cradled her dying husband in her lap with his blood covering her coat and her arms as she sat in a state of shock at the horror that was unfolding. It would be hard for her to forget the tears in Jackie's eyes and her feeling of being unable to do anything for the man in her lap as the car sped toward the hospital with the relentless wailing sound of the sirens all around her. It was a matter of minutes and yet to Jackie those minutes were a lifetime because she knew that he had been shot in the head and she knew what that meant.

"Oh, God, Oh, God," she prayed over and over again, "please don't let this be happening."

For weeks and months afterward, Jackie

would wake at night in a cold sweat having lived through yet another horrendous nightmare as her mind struggled with the events of the morning when Jack had been killed. Time and again the images came back to her and always at night when she was alone in her bed. Throughout the days, weeks and months following his murder, Jackie spent most of the days crying; unable to control the tears that simply flooded from her eyes. And night after night she would awake screaming as the nightmares returned to haunt her. Pills didn't help, sleeping draughts didn't help; it seemed nothing could rid her of these nightmares. And she had no one, save for Jack's younger brother, the wonderful Bobby, to whom she could turn for help. But at night there was no Bobby to save her mind, mop her brow and hold her tight as she suffered yet another moment when the horror returned to her frenzied mind.

Indeed, Jack Kennedy's assassination almost destroyed Jackie. The nightmares never ceased and she came close to losing her sanity. She was certainly deeply depressed and many who knew her well believe she may have contemplated taking her own life because she could see no escape from the horror that had engulfed her entire being. She would sit and weep with people around her and on her own and she would repeat time and again the single word "why?", slowly shaking her head from side to side and unable to come up with an answer to that simple but most profound question.

The Kennedy family nurse, Luella Donavan, who also lost a husband, said that it was not uncommon for a new and young widow to sometimes feel like joining her husband in death because she believes there is nothing left for her to live for. But she believed that Jackie did not go down that path because she realized her two young children needed her desperately.

Bobby Kennedy and Jackie's mother Janet were both of the opinion that the assassination had left Jackie so demoralized and depressed that she might suffer a nervous breakdown. Indeed, Jackie came to say later that in the bleak months following the assassination it was the presence of her children and their need for her that convinced her nothing else in the world mattered more. She believed she only managed to overcome those months of personal anguish and grief because she knew she had to be there for Caroline and John.

Jackie was only 34 at the time of the murder and in desperate need of a shoulder to cry on, someone to support her and care for her. Kenneth P. O'Donnell, Jack Kennedy's tough special assistant, recalled, "Each time I came to see her during the 12 months following Jack's death, she was in tears. Each time I came into the room she would look at me, her eyes filled with tears, and throw her arms around me sobbing on my shoulder. And she looked terrible."

But what made matters worse for Jackie, was that every move she made, every step she took outside her apartment, every ride she took in her car, every place she attended a mob of paparazzi followed, asking questions and flashing cameras in her face. Such treatment at the hands of the press could only make matters worse, but in the months and years following Kennedy's assassination the world wanted to know every tiny detail of her life, her anguish and the fate of her children. And the more the pubescent Athina read about her mother and her relationship with the famous Jackie Kennedy, the more Athina wanted to know about all the relationships.

One year after the assassination, Jackie

Kennedy wrote an emotional tribute to her late husband in *Look* magazine:

> *I don't think there is any consolation. What was lost cannot be replaced. I should have known that it was asking too much to dream that I might have grown old with him and seen our children grow up together. Now I think that I should have known that he was magic all along. I did know it. I should have guessed it could not last ...*

It was, in fact, 18 months since the tragedy before Jackie appeared at a function in public, attending a dance for about 100 people, many of whom were old friends of Jack Kennedy. Reluctantly, Jackie accepted the invitation and, surrounded by friends, she managed to enjoy herself. In the fall of 1965 she even threw a small party at The Sign of the Dove, a restaurant on Third Avenue in New York, and she was seen smiling and happily chatting to her guests as she had done in the good old days when Jack was alive.

From that time onward Jackie began her new life; flying to operas, plays and ballets in the United States and Europe, accepting more invitations to dinners, dances, social events and charity functions. And everywhere she went she was the star. Her looks had returned, her smile charmed everyone, her confidence restored. Gossip in New York was full of the man Jackie would marry when the time was right, after all, the gossips muttered she was only 34 when Jack was killed and she had a life to live. The marriage brokers among New York society were forever making projections, but all the guessing games came to naught, despite some likely protagonists.

To her credit, Jackie didn't enter into such tittle-tattle, preferring to ignore the gossip. Yet, as time would tell, the idea of another man in her life became increasingly less abhorrent. She understood full well that she needed company, needed protection, indeed, needed a man in her life to care for her and the children. And she needed a companion with whom she could grow old gracefully in peace and harmony, rather than a forlorn and lonely widow. Jackie had, however, already decided that she wanted no more children; her beloved two were just fine.

To say that half of New York's high society was taken aback by the news that Ari and Jackie were to marry is a gross understatement. It rocked the cocktail party set and caused the ice to clink in every glass as the rich, the famous and the socialites gulped down their drinks in one shot upon hearing the dramatic news. It also shook Christina.

Ari had never told Alexander or Christina that he was dating Jackie because he never had the confidence to believe that Jackie might one day say yes to the question he was burning to ask her. But even after Jackie agreed to marry him, Ari still waited days to make an announcement, fearing in his heart that she might awaken one morning and tell him she could not go through with the marriage.

In fact, it was after the shooting of Bobby Kennedy in June 1968 that Jackie decided to agree to Ari's proposal because Bobby had been her rock ever since Jack's murder five years before. Now that he was gone there was no one with whom she had the same deep under-standing, no one who understood her and her feelings. And she had sensed that Bobby cared for her and protected her like no one ever had. Out of the blue had stepped Ari Onassis, one of the world's wealthiest men, whom she sensed was kind and understanding, sweet and not too demanding and who appeared to care for her and wanted to protect and shield her from the agonies of life and the ubiquitous press who never left her alone. In truth, those were the real reasons Jackie said yes.

When Athina read of the facts and stories surrounding Ari and Jackie's marriage, she must have been as fascinated as her mother had been some 30 years before when she saw and watched Jackie and her father together. At that time, Christina had already heard of her father's admiration for the Kennedy clan and his wish to become a member of their exclusive society circle. In fact, in the mid-'50s Ari had been romantically linked with Lee Radziwill, Jackie's younger married sister, and she was contemplating divorcing her wealthy husband to marry him. However, Bobby Kennedy heard of the heady romance, stepped in and told Jackie that she must put an immediate end to her sister's idea. She happily obliged and the romance came to an end. It was ironic that only a decade after telling her sister that she must end her romance with Ari Onassis, Jackie also discovered a kindness and generosity so overpowering that she was quite happy to marry him.

There was also another reason why Jackie fled into the arms of Ari Onassis so soon after the assassination of her husband and the murder of her brother-in-law. Jackie was convinced that those who targeted the Kennedys would not stop at Jack and Bobby, but might then turn their hatred to her children. After Bobby's killing an emotional Jackie declared, "I hate this country. I despise America and I don't want my children to live here any more. If they're killing Kennedys, my kids are No. 1 targets. I have to get out of this country."

Ari Onassis had the money to provide the security and protection that Jackie needed for herself and her two children and he had no need to live in the United States.

In October 1968, Jackie married Aristotle in a simple, romantic candlelit ceremony in the tiny chapel set in a cypress grove on Skorpios. Before the wedding, Onassis paid Jackie $3 million and set up a $1 million trust fund for Caroline and John. Also, he had agreed that if he and Jackie were divorced he would pay her an annual sum of $100,000 for the rest of her life.

But Athina's mother Christina believed one of the main reasons Ari fell for Jackie Kennedy was because she reminded him of his own mother, Penelope, who had died when Ari was just 6 years old. As Christina said at the time,

"Jackie's physical attraction for my father was that she had large, round, brown eyes set wide apart, exactly the same face as his own mother."

After their wedding, Ari used to plead with Jackie to comb her dark hair high and to wear a collar of fine lace that covered her neck. On those occasions, Jackie closely resembled Ari's mother in his favorite picture of her. But Ari wasn't looking for a mother substitute. As he viewed it, he had a young, new, sexually wild wife and he was a modern Odysseus. After their wedding Ari boasted to a friend, "Five times a night and twice in the morning; she surpasses all the women I've ever known."

But Jackie, too, had reason to smile. Ari was true to his word and was extraordinarily generous to Jackie during their marriage. It is certainly true that Jackie did enjoy money and her enemies would say that she "loved" money. Facts reveal that there might be some truth in that, but she was prepared to keep her part of the bargain by burnishing Ari's reputation as a great lover and at the same time massaging his pride.

During the first year, estimates suggested that Jackie cost Ari some $20 million — a spending rate of nearly $400,000 a week! Jewelry, clothes, cars, homes, gifts, parties, flights ... everything and anything she wanted. Jackie also kept the money from her second-hand clothes that she sold to a New York store which specialized in designer label hand-me-downs. But Ari didn't know about that. He probably didn't care because she was the prize for which he had craved all his life and he reveled in owning her, because that was how he perceived his wife.

It is not known what Jackie did with the money that came her way but, as a young woman growing up and even while married to Jack Kennedy, she had always been careful with money and she respected it. She was also keen to make sure that when she eventually died there would be sufficient money for both Caroline and John to live the lives of wealthy people. Keeping Ari happy was one way she could make certain that the money kept rolling in.

Later, the magnificent Greek opera singer Maria Callas, his mistress of many years and probably the one woman in the world Ari Onassis ever really loved, would tell of the problems he was having with Jackie after only a year together. Ari would tell her that Jackie used sex all the time, to keep him waiting for one or two nights, to tease him, to flaunt her sexuality in front of him, sometimes dancing seductively in front of him wearing a see-through negligee while guests looked on. And when Ari could take no more teasing Jackie would then give herself to him time after time until he was totally satiated and she was satisfied.

Teenage Athina learned about all of these shenanigans and scandals from the books she read and her young impressionable mind must have raced with the thrill and excitement of the family history. It's expected that the more she read, the more pride Athina felt toward her Greek family, despite the fact that her father Thierry Roussel didn't seem too keen on the Greeks. Athina probably came to believe that her father didn't like Greek people — and yet he had married her mother who was very much a passionate Greek woman.

When still a young girl, Athina wanted only to be like the other girls in her class at school, who were mainly fair-haired and blue eyed. As an adolescent, Athina would put blond streaks in her hair, appearing more Swiss than Greek and her first attempts with makeup made her look more pale than her natural coloring. Athina had inherited the olive skin of her mother and most of her school friends were jealous of its beautiful, delicate shade and their parents would comment on the richness and perfect color of Athina's skin.

Indeed, Athina must have come to believe that they were telling the truth when she discovered the teenage boys looking at her far more than they checked out the other girls in her class. As a result, Athina must have begun to realize that there was a positive side to her Greek ancestry. Despite the problems her father seemed to be having with those Greeks who were taking care of the Onassis family funds, she began feeling proud of being Greek.

Today, Athina thinks of herself as half-Swiss, half-Greek, which is, of course, the case and she doesn't have to make a decision about which nationality to choose because she can enjoy the benefits of being both.

When reading some of the books written about the family, she apparently always put herself in her mother's shoes, wondering what she thought about everything that was going on around her during those years before she was born. Everything she read, Athina must have examined the facts and the happenings as they might have affected her mother, always trying to get inside her mother's mind, wondering whether they thought alike.

Friends say the breakup of the Kennedy-

Onassis marriage intrigued Athina as she felt sure the collapse of that marriage must have intrigued her mother Christina all those years ago.

Perhaps the most important catalyst that triggered the breakdown of the marriage was the tragic death of Ari's son Alexander during take-off from Athens airport in a family seaplane in January 1973. The Piaggio plane he was piloting banked sharply to the right immediately after leaving the ground and crashed within seconds. Alexander, a skilled pilot then 27 years old, survived but suffered horrendous brain damage. After doctors told Ari there was no hope of his ever recovering, he reluctantly gave permission for the life-support system to be switched off. An inquiry showed that the cables controlling the plane's rudders had been incorrectly reconnected during a recent service. Ari, however, was convinced the plane had been sabotaged by his enemies in the CIA and in his anger he vowed to prove it. Of course, he never did.

After her beloved brother's death, Christina, then age 23, began calling Jackie "the black widow" because, she said, "everyone around her dies." It was a cruel nickname, indeed, but there was also a ring of truth in it.

The breakdown in the marriage began when the sexual frisson between the two began to drift away after two years of marriage. In the cruel passage of time it became obvious to Ari's friends that he had literally "bought" Jackie Kennedy's body. He wanted to thrill her and dominate her sexually and he also wanted to show the entire world that the great Aristotle Socrates Onassis had the power, the prestige, the charisma and the sexual attraction to capture the world's most famous and beautiful widow, the former wife of JFK.

Jackie went along with the plan quite happily. She needed protection and she adored money, so she figured that she needed someone with the power and the wealth to care for her, protect her and to spoil her rotten. And Jackie also enjoyed sex.

As she famously told a good female friend, "What the hell. What does it matter if he looks like a gnome? Ari is a great lover."

But there were many other things that Jackie didn't like about Ari and that he, in turn, couldn't stomach about Jackie. Ari would complain that Jackie whined and sulked when they were together. Jackie complained that Ari only wanted to possess her and that he had no real interest in her.

One of their bones of contention arose over Ari's private island of Skorpios, his kingdom, the outcrop of rock where he loved to entertain his friends. Jackie didn't take to his friends, finding most of them old and boring. For the most part, Jackie was bored to death on the island. She hated the food, she didn't like the wine, she didn't get along with the 40 employees on the island and she didn't like the heat of the summer sun that usually lasted some five scorching months. And there was another problem. Jackie was a woman of the television age but Ari wasn't and it was impossible to receive a TV signal on Skorpios. Jackie was reduced to having the latest Hollywood movies sent over from New York. All in all, she wasn't a happy lady.

Those people to whom Jackie confided in her long-distance telephone calls were not surprised when press reports revealed that all was not well with the marriage.

Ari's imagemaker, Nigel Neilson, commented, "Jackie had a whining voice and would sulk if she didn't get her own way. Ari found living with Jackie very difficult. He wasn't used to that type of woman. In essence, he preferred the fiery more passionate Mediterranean-style relationship."

The catalyst for divorce, however, was a note that Jackie had written to her old friend and flame, the handsome, debonair Roswell Gilpatric, the undersecretary of state for welfare in Jack Kennedy's administration, and which Ari read about in newspapers four years after their wedding. Her note read, "Dearest Ros, I wanted to let you know about the wedding before I left, but then everything happened so much more quickly than I'd planned. I hope you know all you were and are and will ever be to me. With all my love, Jackie."

That note spoke volumes. Short, pithy and to the point, it revealed a great deal about Jackie Kennedy and her state of mind when she married Ari Onassis. There could be no mistake that the note was a declaration of an undying love. It also showed that despite what her critics said and wrote about Jackie Kennedy's cool, clinical, icy personality at least with one man, Ros Gilpatric, she was most certainly capable of a deep and loving affair.

The other catalyst was the January 1973 death of his son Alexander, whom he'd always adored. Alexander's death knocked the life out of Ari and he found it difficult to concentrate for some months. He complained that the vision of his beloved Alexander would constantly leap into his mind, confusing his thought pattern. And he would weep, often silently and alone.

So he turned once more to his great love, Maria Callas, and once again they became lovers. However, Ari needed Maria to listen to his rages about Jackie's lack of affection, her moods, her whining, her callous personality and lack of genuine love for him. He also complained about her excessive spending.

During one outburst, Ari fumed, "Every month there are bills, huge bills for me to pay. Only the other month there was one bill, a single bill, for $60,000. And do you know what that was for? I will tell you. It was for 200 pairs of shoes for herself. And that is on top of the huge allowance I give her every month."

He stormed up and down the room as he raged, "And that is just for shoes. I get the same bills every month for handbags, dresses, gowns and coats that would fill a Fifth Avenue shop. It's madness. How could one woman need so many things all the time? I am a rich man, thank God, but this is stupid. What is she doing? Is she mad?"

Jackie continued her wild spending ways as Ari found himself slowing down. He was 73 and feeling old. He was unable to make love to either Jackie or Maria because he always felt so extraordinarily tired. He was diagnosed as suffering from myasthenia, a muscle-wasting disease that causes abnormal fatigue. In the fall of 1974, doctors told him that there was no cure and the strong ox that had been Ari Onassis began to go downhill fast. He died in March the following year.

That left only Athina's mother, Christina, the mother she never really knew and could barely remember, in sole charge of the fabulous Onassis fortune. She would have her work cut out for her.

Chapter Four

Athina has always deeply regretted that her mother died at such a young age. Christina was almost 38 at the time of her death, the young Athina nearly 4 years old and by all accounts a precocious, happy little girl. In reality, however, Athina barely knew her mother and today she has few memories of what her mother was like. Of course, Athina has seen many photographs of her mother and today, at age 18.

There is no doubt that Athina is a far better-looking young woman than her mother ever was with her large, droopy eyes and close family resemblance to her father's features.

Like her father, poor Christina was always overweight and hated it. She never liked her body and would sometimes tell her lovers that she wished she was more beautiful, not for herself but for them. However, as the world knew only too well, Christina had other attractions that brought lovers flocking to her side, the small matter of a few billion dollars. The money helped and Christina knew it. She readily used her wealth to attract men.

Her handsome Argentine lover Luis Basualdo told the story of how he had once asked Christina whether she would prefer to be beautiful and poverty-stricken or less beautiful and wealthy. As a joke, Christina had first replied that she would prefer to be beautiful and wealthy, changed that to less beautiful and wealthy but finally decided upon being beautiful and poverty-stricken.

"Why?" Luis asked her.

"If I was beautiful and poverty-stricken," she replied candidly, "I would simply marry a rich man or take rich lovers."

That conversation became more serious and Christina told Basualdo, one of the two men in her life that she really loved, "Life for a rich woman is always very difficult. You can never tell whether a man wants you or just your money. The only way out of that conundrum is to only date and marry rich men, but I can't find any rich handsome men who I want to spend time with. I have found most rich men are more interested in their money than in their wives. And I wouldn't want that."

Yet to Athina the child, money meant nothing. She grew up assuming her father was wealthy because she had no idea that all the money he was spending, all the luxuries the family were enjoying, really came from her and the incredible fortune she had inherited. She just believed that her beloved father was simply rich, generous and kind, and she loved him.

As Athina matured from childhood to adolescence she must have begun to wonder what life would have been like growing up with her own "Mama." She only had vague memories. She could recall meeting many other children whom her mother would invite to play at their Swiss home Boislande. Indeed, Christina would invite other mothers to bring their babies to the house from the time Athina was just a few weeks old. And these visits would generally take place three or four times a week, primarily because

Christina was convinced that her darling Athina should grow up in a family atmosphere learning social skills from a young age.

As a result, Athina became a sociable little girl, friendly with six or seven boys and girls of her age, whom she would look forward to seeing almost on a daily basis. Christina would invite the mothers and their children to a meal or a picnic in the garden because she believed in the Greek tradition of members of families and extended families frequently meeting at the home of grandparents for meals with all the children present. But there were very few other memories for the richest girl in the world.

But with the sudden and unexpected death of her mother, the Greek influence on her life disappeared overnight. It seems that her father was glad to be rid of the Greek influence on his daughter, preferring to bring her up and educate her as though she was a little French girl living in Switzerland. As the years went by, the only Greek culture and influence that Athina encountered were her few memories of childhood and, as the years passed, those memories were fast disappearing.

She had no idea that Christina spoiled her rotten. Even before she was born Christina, who knew she was expecting a baby girl, spent a small fortune buying designer baby clothes for her darling daughter. In fact, most of the clothes were designed exclusively for Athina by Dior, but the little girl had no idea they were anything special. Throughout the few years they were together, Christina would change Athina's clothes three or five times a day and every article of clothing — except for diapers — bore a designer label.

Perhaps it was fortunate for Athina that she had little or no idea that she was being spoiled. She probably grew up believing that every little girl had to have her clothes changed four or more times a day, in the same way that she grew up believing that every home had nurses, nannies, maids and servants. It was her childhood, her life and to her that was normality.

It was an accident of good fortune for Athina that her mother had insisted that her father Thierry Roussel spend much of his time at Boislande so that their beloved daughter would grow up knowing both her parents. Christina was very much against one-parent families because she believed such families harmed the children. More importantly, Christina had learned from her own bitter experience that children were happiest when those parents loved each other, lived together and both loved the child.

Christina had realized from a very early age that she was an unwanted child, seemingly unwanted by both her mother and her father. She grew up closer to nannies and maids than her own parents who, in many respects, simply deserted her from the moment of her birth. Indeed, Athina would learn much later, Christina was fortunate, if not lucky, to have ever arrived in the world.

When Christina's mother, Tina, who was half-British, half-Greek, told her husband Ari Onassis that she was pregnant again, Ari tried to persuade her to have an abortion. Tina readily agreed and an abortion was arranged. This would have been Tina's third abortion since giving birth to Alexander only two years earlier. However, Tina was only 21 and she didn't want to jeopardize any future relationships with any future husband or lover. Tina told Ari, who was nearly 30 years older than she, that she was going to have the baby she was expecting.

At first, Ari accepted his wife's decision but secretly he had no wish for another child. Why the great Aristotle Onassis didn't want any more children is not certain, although there have been many suggestions put forward. The favored reason is that Ari wanted no family quarrels over his burgeoning fortune because he reasoned fortunes only divided families, setting children against each other and making for unhappy, jealous and miserable relationships.

As the months passed, Ari became more irate that his young wife would not get rid of the unborn child because she offered him no explanation why she wanted to have the baby. As Ari noticed Tina's abdomen expanding, he became even more irate, constantly demanding, "Why not get rid of it? Why not get rid of it? You got rid of the others, what's so special about this one?"

Ari convinced himself that the reason she wanted to keep the baby was because it was not his baby but that of a lover. He convinced himself that Tina no longer fancied her "old man" or wanted to have sex with him anymore but lusted after younger, more virile, handsome men. That thought struck at the very heart of Ari's belief in himself and infuriated him because he could not conceive of the possibility of his young beautiful wife ever contemplating sex with another man. He demanded to know the name of her lover, shouting, screaming at his wife, ordering her to tell him the truth and name the lover.

The possibility that his wife might have a lover also invigorated Ari and he would demand sex with Tina four or five times a day to prove that he was a great lover. Understandably, Tina complained, telling Ari that having sex so often when pregnant was uncomfortable. Ari refused to believe her, suggesting she was only saying that because she preferred her unknown lover who, he presumed, was both young and handsome. In fact, Tina did not have a lover and told Ari a thousand times that there was no other man in her life. But Ari refused to believe her and the bullying and demands for sex continued.

However, Tina had no wish to tell her husband the truth. Though young, Tina was bright and intelligent and she knew it was unlikely their marriage would last because they had little or nothing in common and they spent much of their lives living in different countries. Another point was that Tina no longer fancied Ari and his constant sexual demands only turned her further against him.

Tina would tell her close friends, "I hate Ari making love to me because he simply uses me and he abuses me. There is no love, no love at all. He's like an animal and I really do believe he likes to hurt me. Sometimes, it's really painful but he won't take no for an answer."

Perhaps Ari feared his beautiful, young Tina would find another lover and leave him and that really would have hurt his pride. Throughout his life Ari played the role of a macho man, a stud in the bed and a gentle and romantic lover-seducer of the women who attracted him. And, of course, the attractive Tina certainly caught the eye of many young men. She hoped and prayed that one day she and Ari would divorce and she would then find another, younger man whom, she presumed, might also want children. But Tina couldn't tell Ari any of this.

As the pregnancy wore on, Ari became

angrier by the day and Tina became more alarmed. Ari would stand in front of her as she sat in a chair or lay resting on the bed and he would shout and yell at her, the veins in his neck standing out, his eyes glazed over in anger, his mouth spitting saliva as he remonstrated with his hands gesticulating in frustration and anger at his wife's refusal to have an abortion.

One day Ari went too far. He beat her with his fists, ferociously and hard, punching her all over her body but especially raining blows on her abdomen, while Tina fought desperately to protect the baby in her womb. It was a vile, despicable and shocking attack that revealed the depths Aristotle Onassis could sink in his personal relations. Worse still, the attack was not simply in frustration or anger but because his wife refused to obey his will and have an abortion. Tina was certain that his ferocious attack on her was a deliberate and calculated bid to bring on a miscarriage. She told her future lover, the handsome young Venezuelan Reinaldo Herrera, "There was so much blood spilled on the carpet that the stain could never be washed away. The carpet finally had to be replaced."

But Ari's brutal attack failed. A few months

later, in December 1950, Tina gave birth to a bouncing, well-developed baby girl, Athina's mother, Christina. She was unharmed.

Tina tried to be a good mother to both Alexander and Christina, but she found life increasingly difficult with the tempestuous, arrogant husband who demanded that his young wife should be the perfect hostess, entertaining his rich and famous friends in their magnificent villa, the Chateau de la Croe, on the French Riviera. But she could not cope with Ari's demands for her to be the perfect wife of the world's richest man, dressing immaculately, looking stunning, organizing parties and dinners to perfection and being sagacious and witty with all his guests, most of whom were twice her age.

As a result of Ari's constant nagging and his inherent ability to put her down, Tina lost confidence in herself not only as a hostess but also as a mother. She had tried to be a kind and loving mother, but felt she was not cut out for motherhood. It was Alexander and Christina who suffered. When Christina was 3 years old, poor Tina suffered a mild nervous breakdown, which enraged Ari still more. Thus, Alexander and Christina grew up with a rather pathetic, nervous mother who had no confidence. Nor did their mother have the strength of character to stand up to her bullying husband, who had little time for his children, especially his baby daughter.

Christina arrived in the world just as Aristotle was reaching the pinnacle of his ambitions. In 1954, he bought a magnificent 325-foot yacht and renamed it *Christina* after his daughter. Also, he moved his headquarters to Monaco, where he would run his fast-growing fleet of shipping tankers. Ari decided to live and work from the *Christina,* with its nine state rooms, and Alexander and Christina lived there, too. But Ari would only see the children for a few minutes each day and they grew up almost alone, cut off from the real world with no friends to play with.

That was the principal reason why Christina was determined that young Athina would always have plenty of playmates her own age — because of the experiences of her own childhood brought up in an adult world with no other children to share her life. It wasn't surprising that later in her life Christina would tell people, "I've been an adult since I was 9."

When Athina became a teenager and began

reading the occasional biographies of Ari, Jackie Kennedy and her mother Christina, she must have compared herself favorably to photographs of her mother and take note of descriptions, so happy that she had not been born with all of her mother's features. She would read of her mother as a teenager being described as ugly with a prominent nose, dark, deep circles around her eyes, an odd, awkward girl who always looked sad. Reading of such problems her mother had to contend with, friends say that Athina was determined to smile and look happy.

But it wasn't only her mother's looks that Athina read about. She understood from a young age that her mother had left her a fortune which, one day, would all be hers. Athina learned from the biographies that her mother never showed any anxiety about the great wealth that she would one day inherit. Athina decided to adopt the same approach. She was enjoying her life too much as a teenager to worry about such problems; they could wait until she was older.

Though Athina probably didn't comprehend her reaction to her inheritance, she was fortunate that she had followed her mother's same attitude because she grew up as a remarkably self-confident, but modest and levelheaded, young woman with no arrogance or pretensions. Her family, her school friends and her pony were far more important to her than money. Athina was a popular girl among school friends, especially those who also loved riding and ponies. Athina loved to spend time after school as well as most weekends at the nearby stables, grooming her pony, talking horses and chatting to the other girls.

In the tradition of Greek ship owners, Christina had left virtually everything to her only surviving direct descendant, her young daughter. The island of Skorpios, the Villa Crystal in Switzerland, the fabulous apartment in the Avenue Foch in Paris were all to be retained until Athina reached the age of 18. Before her death, Christina, on advice, had sold her father's entire tanker fleet netting some $130 million, which was to be invested for Athina. Her financial advisers were given the task of investing this fortune as they saw fit so that by age 18 the young Athina would inherit a fortune of at least $1 billion U.S. dollars.

More important to the growing Athina was the fact that her stepmother would prove to

Athina, age 18, as she pursues her dream of a place
on the 2004 Greek Olympic equestrian team.

Aristotle Onassis with his wife Tina and their young children, Alexander and Christina.

The wedding that shocked the world – Jackie and Caroline Kennedy ride away from the ceremony with Ari.

During his marriage to Jackie, Ari took his role as stepfather to young John Kennedy Jr. seriously, spending more time with John than he ever did with his own son, Alexander. They are shown here in NYC in 1969.

Aristotle and Christina Onassis – Christina adored her father, but he seldom had time for her. That is, until six months after the death of Alexander, when he decided she needed to learn to direct his vast business empire. That's when she proved she was her father's daughter.

Jackie and Ari aboard the yacht "Christina." Onassis provided Jackie with the security she needed after the assassination of RFK.

At Ari's funeral in 1975, Christina (above right) snubbed Jackie (back left with John Jr.), calling her the "black widow" and blaming her for the deaths of her brother and father.

Christina wed Alexander Andreadis a few months after her father's death. The marriage lasted just six months.

Christina enjoyed partying at the infamous Studio 54 in 1977. She thrived in that debauched atmosphere.

Then and now – Christina (above) and Athina (right). Like mother, like daughter? Only time will tell.

Sergei Kauzov weds Christina in 1978 – however, this
was one more marriage that was not meant to last. She
used the fact that he was a KGB agent to divorce him,
aware that single detail was enough to bankrupt the
vast Onassis shipping business during the Cold War.

Young and handsome, Thierry Roussel swept Christina off her feet, but it was 10 years after their first fling that they finally married. Not quite a year later, Athina was born.

Throughout her life, Christina struggled with her weight and took a variety of diet pills to help combat the problem.

Proud papa Thierry with baby Athina.

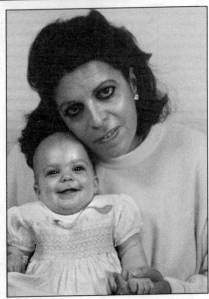

A very happy baby Athina with her mother — who would die mysteriously when Athina was just 3 years old.

Athina was doted upon by her mother. Christina not only showered her with extraordinary material gifts, but she loved to spend time with her baby daughter.

In 1990 Thierry married his longtime live-in love
and mother of his other children, Gaby. Athina
was a flower girl at the wedding.

At long last, Athina's first trip to Greece in 1998 with her father, stepmom Gaby and their children. The Greek people adored Athina. However, the Roussels were there for Thierry to pursue his legal wranglings with the Onassis Foundation.

Athina and Doda — the boyfriend 12 years her senior. Just as her mother Christina did not care about the marital or financial status of the men who interested her, neither has Athina.

be a remarkably good and stable influence surrogate. Marianne "Gaby" Landhage was a beautiful Swedish translator who had moved to Paris and, with her high cheek bones, blond hair and near-perfect body was snapped up as a model by French photographers. She was only 20 years old when she first met Thierry Roussel, who was two years her senior, and they soon became lovers. Throughout his 20s Roussel's love for Gaby was the single most important stabilizing influence on his wild young life. Gaby was not his only lover, but he would always return to her. It seems that Gaby accepted this relationship, unperturbed by her lover's comings and goings.

In his book *The Life of Christina Onassis*, William Wright would write, "Gaby was a ravishingly beautiful blonde, with high cheek bones and the finely etched features of a Garbo. She was also, by all accounts, exceptionally good-hearted and kind, an unaffected woman with her feet squarely on the ground in a solid, particularly Swedish sort of way. Despite the recherché Parisian worlds to which her remarkable looks gave Landhage access, her head was never turned by the glamour or high life. Her feelings for Roussel were total and, in the estimation of her friends, unencumbered with extraneous ambitions."

When Gaby became bored with the life of modeling while waiting for Roussel to marry her, she left Paris and returned to Sweden, enrolling in a management course before taking a job with a cosmetics firm in Malmo. Despite his reticence to pop the question, Roussel was still apparently in love with Gaby but not sufficiently so to put an end to his life of freedom and to settle down and marry her. Instead, Roussel bought her a small house in Sweden where she could settle down and he would visit her from time to time. The patient, tolerant and unflappable Gaby accepted the situation and waited.

While she as reading, Athina probably came to understand and realize how fortunate she had been in having Gaby as her stepmother, someone who happily accepted Athina as though she was her own daughter, treating her in exactly the same way as she treated her own children, giving Athina the same motherly love and devotion that she gave Erik, Sandrine and Johanna.

And Athina was given exactly the same education as Gaby's children in a good Swiss school that was attended by all the other middle-class children of Swiss parentage. At school, Athina received the same work, the same discipline, the same encouragement, the same workload as every other child. She was given no privileges and no special attention. The only difference was that two SAS-trained special forces bodyguards were always in attendance. They were always armed but their presence was discreet. Within a very short time, the bodyguards were accepted as part of the school furniture not only by the teachers and the parents but also by the children, who would wave to them whenever they met, usually when arriving or leaving school each day. The bodyguards were selected not only on their professional expertise but also on their characters and personality because the Roussels wanted happy, relaxed, smiling men around their home, not simply tough, hard men wanting to prove themselves.

Athina proved a bright, intelligent girl who appeared to enjoy her school days. She readily took part in class discussions, showed enthusiasm to learn whatever subjects she was studying and was diligent in handing in her work on time. Athina showed a good grasp of two vitally important subjects —

languages and math. Teachers spoke of her natural ability to grasp languages and today she speaks fluent English, French, Swedish and Italian and has a good grasp of Greek. She also showed a certain aptitude for art.

Athina also enjoyed school sports, playing netball and hockey, learning to swim and being coached in tennis lessons. She developed into a strong swimmer, one reason being that she inherited strong thigh and leg muscles from her mother, which meant she won many school swimming races. Athina took great pleasure being a good athlete because she knew that games, athletics and swimming had nothing whatsoever to do with wealth. At sports she was accepted by teachers and pupils alike as an enthusiastic and successful athlete and she reveled in the acclamation from her school pals. Athletics gave Athina the self-confidence she needed.

However, those school sports were all but forgotten when Athina decided that riding would become her one and only interest. Indeed, her interest soon became a consuming passion. It seemed that nothing else mattered to her. Athina fell in love with ponies and riding. And they have been a vital part of her life for 10 years.

When Athina first came to fully understand that Gaby was not her real mother, she probably became jealous of the other girls in her class because she was different. Gaby would remind Athina that she did have a mother whom she had known as a young girl but unfortunately she had died. That was the sole reason why she had come to live with her and her father, Thierry. But that didn't stop Athina wanting Gaby to be her mother so that she could be just the same as all her school friends. She just hated being different.

Quiet, unobtrusive appeals were made to the parents of the other children in Athina's class to treat Athina in the same way as they would any other child. They urged the parents to invite Athina to their homes to play with their children so that she would feel that her life was no different. And the parents responded kindly, always including Athina in birthday parties and as she grew older she would be invited to stay overnight. In turn, Gaby would invite Athina's friends back to her home.

It is difficult to exaggerate how important a part Gaby has played in Athina's life thus far. She has provided Athina with a remarkable degree of love and stability, support and kindly discipline, enabling Athina to become a stable, self-assured, happy young woman on the threshold of a life that will be full of opportunities. To those I have spoken, all tell how Athina had developed into a calm, self-confident and independent young woman seemingly ready to confront the many problems she will soon face as the wealthiest young woman in the world.

As one mature woman remarked, "Athina looks you straight in the eye when you chat with her. She has no fear, nothing to hide and seems confident beyond her years, which shows that the family life provided by Gaby has given her a quiet self-confidence though she is never brash, arrogant or conceited. Bringing up the world's wealthiest girl, the granddaughter of someone like Ari Onassis, cannot have been the easiest job for any woman. And yet, it seems that Gaby was the perfect person to do so because she is so calm and cool about everything, never flying off the handle, never seemingly exasperated or angry about anything but, instead, always exuding a quiet confidence that Athina seems to have adopted for her own character. She really has done a wonderful job as her stepmother."

Despite the furor that has been created

from time to time by those Greek lawyers, businessmen and financial advisers responsible for managing Athina's fortune, there are some members of the extended Onassis family now living in Greece who believe that the death of her mother at such a young age was certainly untimely but may perhaps have been beneficial to her daughter.

There are many who will admit that being in the care and protection of Gaby has given Athina the start in life that she would never have experienced if her mother had not died at such a young age. Poor Christina, with her melancholy and her failure to find emotional satisfaction or lasting happiness, would probably not have been capable of providing Athina with the same emotional stability and calm background that she found in the home of Gaby and Thierry Roussel and their children.

In a nutshell, Christina was reared in the most incredible luxury with parents who didn't want her and starved her of love and affection. She had an overbearing father whom she adored but rarely saw and a mother who found her social life infinitely more important than her daughter's needs. She lost her darling brother in a fluke air crash, followed in quick succession by the death of her mother of a drug overdose and then the death of her aging father to a fatal illness. At the age of 24, Christina found herself alone in the world as the sole heir to the fabulous Onassis fortune and one of the richest women in the world.

Athina learned from reading biographies of the mother she never really knew that Christina was beset with personal problems that she found difficult to cope with. Athina learned that her mother suffered from a chronic weight problem which gnawed at her very fiber, undermining her self-confidence, destroying any vestiges of self-esteem.

Early on, Christina hated her body with a passion. She suffered from violent mood swings that she believed stemmed from the drugs she was taking to control the weight she couldn't lose. Her four marriages all failed, including her last, to the man who fathered her darling Athina and who gave her life a semblance of normalcy. But even the arrival of Athina failed to stem her mood swings and melancholy. Her short and turbulent life, her depths of despair and her desperate need to find a man who truly and completely loved her proved problematic and elusive. And, in many respects, the fabulous fortune she inherited never helped her find the happiness and calm for which she craved.

Yet in her reading, Athina must have found a ray of hope in the latter stages of her mother's life, which could give her some expectation and confidence that her life might not be so difficult and tragic as her mother's had been. It was her mother's apparent natural business acumen that she had learned from her father. It was six months after the death of her brother Alexander that her father decided that 22-year-old Christina, as the only surviving Onassis, must learn the rudiments of the vast family enterprise — shipping.

At first, however, Aristotle's attempts to personally educate his daughter were not successful because, though he may have been a brilliant businessman, he did not possess the patience to be a good teacher. The two would argue, which upset both of them so her father decided to abandon that plan. Instead, he asked one of his senior managers, Costa Gratsos, who ran the Onassis New York offices of Olympic Maritime situated in Fifth Avenue to be her mentor.

Athina's mother was determined to show her father that she was bright, intelligent, hard-working and a good student. Each day she would arrive at 9 a.m. at the New York office and work assiduously, take only one hour for lunch, and work through until 5 or 6 p.m. The staff was impressed with her rapid understanding of the complexities of the shipping business and she won their appreciation when she asked to be moved to the general office staffed by dozens of young women rather than working in an office of her own. She also impressed the staff at Frank B. Hall, the ship-insurance brokers for whom Onassis was the most highly valued client.

Within a year, Onassis heard from his New York directors that his daughter was grasping the essentials of the shipping empire and the complexities of the ship-insurance business so quickly that he decided to take her under his own wing again, taking her with him to meet their company's most important international clients such as Shell and British Petroleum.

It was her mother's remarkable grasp and command of the Onassis shipping empire after her father's death in 1975 that proved a dramatic and invigorating example for the teenage Athina. At that time, the world oil-tanker business was in the worst slump of its history with no anticipated improvement. Huge losses faced the Onassis shipping line with its 50 tankers; his Olympic Airlines was virtually bankrupt due to the huge rise in the cost of oil after the Arab-Israeli war of 1973; his venture into New York property was losing money and there were serious problems facing the Onassis bank in Switzerland.

Worse still, Onassis had bequeathed a complicated will that put little faith in his daughter's ability to run the empire. But Aristotle hadn't realized his own daughter's prodigious determination, her iron will and her remarkable, seemingly natural, business acumen. With the help of family lawyers, she seized control of the shipping empire, driven by her determination to prove her father wrong. In the process, the young, inexperienced Christina appeared to have inherited her father's ruthless business acumen by agreeing to Jackie Kennedy Onassis' demands for $26 million on the condition that Jackie surrender all rights to the shipping empire. Jackie also agreed to part with her share of Skorpios and the famous *Christina* yacht.

And Athina's respect for her mother must have continued unabated as she read how

Christina had immediately flown to see and talk to the shipping companies' most important clients in the United States, Europe and the Far East, telling them all, "In the future, if anyone wants to do business with our companies, they will have to speak to me."

Christina was proving herself, showing extraordinary willpower and vigor as well as a remarkable grasp of the problems facing the empire, but still the lawyers and the directors at the top of the Onassis empire, as well as other Greek ship owners doubted whether her remarkable initial grasp of the huge business had been a fluke or whether this young, inexperienced and unpredictable woman still in her 20s had indeed inherited the brilliant business brain of her legendary father.

At age 18, it's likely that Athina was beginning to wonder whether she would one day run the Onassis business of which she knew absolutely nothing. Athina had never even met the people who ran her empire and cared for her billions. And she knew there was tons of money invested somewhere because her mother had seen to that. Whether by foresight, good luck or brilliant business sense, Christina had also chosen the right moment to dispose of the great majority of the Onassis shipping fleet in deals that netted her billions of dollars, investing the lot in property and government stock.

Athina appears determined that she now wants to learn more about the Onassis empire, the investments and, more importantly, to meet the people who ran the empire. She had already learned from her books that her beloved father Thierry and those who ran the empire had been at loggerheads for years. But she had no idea why. She decided to find out.

Chapter Five

From age 11 Athina began to understand that she was different from all the other children at the unpretentious Swiss state school she attended in the quiet, picturesque village of Lussy-sur-Morges near Lausanne on the shores of Lake Geneva. She appeared to accept that the tough-looking former British SAS bodyguards who went to school with her each day, inconspicuously hung around the playground and then took her back home in the afternoon were part of her life and she came to treat them as her friends. She seemed to like them and their sense of humor, she joked with them, played ball games with them and never fully understood why it was necessary for these men to be a part of her life every day. They also lived in a small single-story bungalow on the estate where she lived with her parents and other siblings.

But the SAS bodyguards were always dressed casually, often in T-shirts and jeans and never wore any style of official uniform. To Athina they must have seemed just ordinary guys she would see in the village, but she knew they always carried handguns. She realized that they were always not far away from her, their job was to take care of her, protect her, look after her in case someone tried to kidnap her or take her away. As she grew older, Athina undeniably became more confident that these men who looked after her were men she could trust. Hadn't they always told her, "We're here just to look after you because you're a very special little girl."

She had liked hearing that because it not only made Athina feel good, but it also meant that she always felt safe and protected because these men were there to look after her year round. They surely gave Athina a certain confidence, a protective sense of warmth and well-being.

No matter what she did, where she went or whom she met she was secure in the knowledge that they would always be there to protect and look after her. It also must have made some of the other girls at school jealous, because they understood that Athina Onassis Roussel was no ordinary girl but someone special. As the children grew older, however, they would soon learn from their parents that Athina had to be protected because she was the wealthiest little girl in the world.

As a result, some of her school friends treated Athina with deference, others were jealous of her but, fortunately for Athina, she got along reasonably well with most of her school friends. Of course, she also had some special close friends.

But during her early teenage years, Athina probably hadn't fully realized that her life wasn't that simple. Her darling stepmother Gaby and the father she adored had done all in their power to ensure that Athina was brought up just like their other children, just like any of the other girls at school, just like the other girls she knew from the village. They wanted Athina to have as normal an upbringing as possible, though they fully realized that as she grew older she would have to come to understand that she was an exceptional young woman solely because her mother and her grandfather happened to be very rich and they had left her all their money.

In an effort to educate Athina, encourage her to understand her special privileged position as well as to introduce her to the lifestyle she would one day enjoy, her stepmother Gaby gently let her know that the privilege of having lots of money also brought with it responsibilities. They wanted her to understand that money didn't grow on trees but that the fortune she would one day inherit had been earned by the sheer hard work of her grandfather and of her mother. Repeatedly, the sensible Gaby would tell her stepdaughter, "Waste not, want not."

Gaby knew only too well what extraordinary wealth had done for Christina, believing that for all intents and purposes, her fantastic fortune had brought her no lasting happiness, no confidence and no self-assurance. Indeed, Gaby believed from the conversations she had with Christina that her life was full of a multitude of personal problems that made her depressed and, often, really miserable. Gaby also believed that Christina's wealth had brought her a string of lovers, many of whom she believed seemed more intent on dating

Christina simply because she was wealthy and they fancied enjoying some time living the life of the idle rich and being spoiled rotten.

In return, so Gaby understood, the men provided male company for which Christina yearned, as well as frequent sexual enjoyment, and on occasions even sexual fulfillment. But more often than not, Christina discovered that the sex came with little or no real deep-seated affection. All in all, Gaby believed Christina had led a sad life and, fortunately for Athina, Gaby believed it was her responsibility to try to bring up Athina in a happy, loving family atmosphere, to give her the confidence and self-assurance to lead a full life which would be far happier and satisfying than her mother had ever enjoyed.

To that end, Gaby had sought to provide Athina with exactly the same life as any other reasonably wealthy Swiss family but she would try to make sure she didn't spoil Athina or permit her to believe she had a privileged life different from any of her school friends. To those in the village who have grown up with Athina it seems that Gaby has succeeded in her determination to give Athina a stable, happy home life.

From age 12, Athina was given weekly pocket money of 200 Swiss francs ($120 dollars). With that money she would buy Spice Girls and Madonna tapes, food for her pet rabbit, tidbits for the love of her life — her 14.5-hand Arab pony Arco — and biscuits for her yellow Labrador retriever Nicky. She would also buy teen magazines as well as English and French magazines specializing in ponies, show-jumping and eventing. For reading, Athina liked stories and books about teenage girls and their ponies.

Athina is fluent in French, English, Italian and Swedish, but Greek, the native tongue of both her mother and her famous grandfather, is virtually nonexistent. Indeed, that was one of the bones of contention between Thierry Roussel and the Greek lawyers who were responsible under the terms of her mother's will for ensuring the Onassis family fortune continued to grow until Athina became 21.

At that age Athina can then choose whether she wants to be a part of the business empire, work in some part of the business or, one day perhaps, assume complete control and command of the worldwide Onassis complex of investments — from property to shipping, hedge funds to retail shops. On the other hand, if she doesn't want to be involved in the day-to-day running of the Onassis empire, she can simply leave the command and control of the various businesses in the hands of Onassis directors and the family lawyers who will invest her wealth in suitable projects, companies, financial institutions or whatever and, in return for a handsome fee, work to provide her with an income that befits the world's richest young woman.

Athina's Swiss upbringing, however, tended to negate her Greek ancestry, which would have undoubtedly saddened both her mother and enraged her grandfather. Indeed, Christina hoped the young Athina would feel the same pride in the citizenship of her native land as she and her whole family had done during their lifetimes.

It was sometime around her 15th birthday that Athina came to understand that a feud had been raging since her childhood between her beloved father and those Greek trustees of the fortune her mother had bequeathed to her. The adolescent Athina probably wanted nothing to do with the legal turmoil over the Onassis fortune. It was something seemingly beyond her control of which she had little or no interest.

Importantly, Athina had come to trust her father absolutely. She knew nothing of his earlier financial disasters and failures as a businessman and entrepreneur; she had no idea that her Greek trustees treated her father as little more than a greedy gold digger who allegedly only took Athina into his home to try and extract more of the Onassis fortune from the fund and deposit it into his own bank accounts.

It was at this time that Athina informed the four Athens-based trustees that she did not want any relationship or contact with the Greek members of the board of trustees. By virtue of Christina's last will and testament, Thierry Roussel was excluded from the administration of his daughter's estate, which was entrusted to a five-member board, making decisions by a majority vote. As Athina's father, Thierry Roussel had a seat on the board as a simple member with no voting rights.

As Athina was growing up, however, she had no idea that her father was constantly challenging her mother's will through the courts — right up to the highest court, demanding that all the income earned by Athina's inheritance from her family and their estate should be acquired by him personally until Athina reached age 18. He also demanded that a major part of the administration of her inheritance should be entrusted to him. Athina also didn't know that her father's claims failed all the way through the courts and the income remained in Athina's inherited assets. The administration of the inheritance was exercised by the board appointed by her mother in her will.

In August 1999, however, when Athina was 15, a Swiss court removed the entire board, including Roussel, and replaced it with a third party. They ruled that Thierry Roussel was to be removed because, in the court's opinion, he had personal claims against his daughter's inheritance. The Greek members were removed because they had disputes with Athina's father and, most importantly, because young Athina did not wish the administration of her inheritance to be exercised by the Greeks as "she feels a great abhorrence to anything which is Greek, although she is aware that her mother, her grandfather and the estate are Greek. She wished the Greeks to be out of her life."

Understandably, the board members were furious with the judgment because they believed that, as they had feared, Thierry

Roussel had used his close involvement in Athina's upbringing to influence her against all things Greek and had come to persuade her that she wanted nothing whatsoever to do with the Greek trustees that Roussel always referred to as "Graybeards."

To those Greeks still employed by the foundations, employed on the Onassis island of Skorpios and employed in the great majority of positions of power and influence in the extended Onassis empire, this damning indictment of all Greek people involved in her life came as a stunning blow. That single quotation from Athina spelled out by the Swiss court also exacerbated the enmity toward Thierry Roussel by not only the Graybeards but everyone involved in the Onassis empire. However, the board dismissed Athina's outrageous statement, stating that it had probably been made at her father's instigation and his advice.

To those Onassis employees at all levels, there was a genuine concern for Athina remaining under the influence of her father, who appeared to be driven by an unnatural hunger to take much of Athina's inheritance and income under his own wing. From their standpoint, the only possible reason could be that Roussel was little more than a fortune-hunter who had accidentally fathered Athina and was now intent on stripping as much money as possible from his beloved daughter's inheritance.

Apparently as a result of that dramatic court case, Athina decided to find out more about her background, her parents, her forefathers, the people who had created the fortune she would one day inherit. It was about this time that she began to read books about her extraordinary family of which she was the last remaining descendant. And as she grew older and understood more the value of money, the more interest she showed in the Onassis empire.

One can only imagine that Athina desperately wanted to give all the support she could to her father; she was only too happy to go along with his wishes and permit him to take care of all the inheritance and the Onassis empire because she had such faith in him. Hadn't her father being battling the Graybeards on her behalf? Hadn't he been fighting long, complicated court cases on her behalf? Hadn't he always told her that he would do everything in his power to care for her and protect her? Hadn't he always told her that he only wanted the best for her? Understandably, Athina had come to believe in her father absolutely; he could do no wrong. To Athina he was the one person she trusted to care for her affairs and she wanted him to control it all.

But no one knows whether Thierry had told his daughter of his own disastrous investments and financial failures. Thierry Roussel had grown up as a rich young Parisian kid whose family had founded France's largest pharmaceutical company, which had been partially nationalized by the French government. The family had retained a 40 percent stake but Thierry's father Henri, a ladies' man, had sold his share to a brother and had used his fortune to enjoy a life among the rich and famous in Kenya and Marbella, Spain.

Thierry had attended one of France's most exclusive schools and he soon began to portray the family trait of enjoying beautiful women and acting in an extroverted manner, particularly in front of young women. Intelligent, quick-witted, handsome, athletic and good-looking with blue eyes and blond hair, Thierry was the darling of the Mediterranean jet-set of the 1970s, enjoying life in the Greek islands, the French Riviera and Marbella.

Thierry also enjoyed the more exotic and dangerous sports such as power boating, big-game hunting and helicopter skiing. He also lived well, exuding wealth he didn't really have. He lived in an apartment in the smartest part of Paris with three personal servants and used the family's rundown villa south of Paris as his personal country estate. In his mid-20s, he set out to make his fortune in the knowledge that his father would probably have spent his dwindling resources by the time of his death.

Thierry became involved in an advertising agency, a home furnishing company, a publishing house and, to no one's surprise, a modeling agency. Apparently, some of his ventures were quite successful but others ended with losses. At the time he and Christina got together in 1983, Thierry was in financial trouble, having sold his interest in the modeling agency at a $3 million loss and a disastrous land venture in Africa with losses greater than $10 million.

Christina fell instantly in love with the handsome, blond, jet-set Thierry and within a few months they were married. Within weeks, Thierry was delving into his bride's various business firms and company, examining the accounts and talking to personnel as though he now owned his bride's empire. He discovered she was living below her income, spending only $6 million a year from her annual income of some $50 million.

So Thierry set about altering some things. On his advice, Christina ditched her old Lear jet and bought a $15 million Falcon 50; bought a larger apartment in London for $2 million, and for their new base in Switzerland, Thierry advised Christina to buy a beautiful 18-room villa set on 10 acres of landscaped gardens in Gingins, near Geneva, overlooking Lake Leman, at a cost of $5 million.

Within months, however, it seemed Christina was handing over large parcels of her wealth to Thierry and within the space of a few years her financial advisers estimated she had given him $50 million! Before she died in 1988, however, Christina confessed that she had given Thierry $73 million.

While Christina was still alive and married to Thierry, her lawyers feared that he was actively trying his damnedest to take command of his wife's fortune and run the family business. He would make statements to the effect that he was no longer happy with handouts from Christina but wanted a major say in managing his wife's business affairs. Warnings were discreetly given to Christina but her lawyers were well aware that to her, money meant nothing compared to having a handsome man to love her. The extended Onassis family, however, had been well aware of what was happening — that her inheritance and the Onassis family fortune appeared to be diminishing fast and furiously and all the money seemed to be going to Thierry Roussel.

On one famous occasion at a nightclub in St. Moritz, the topic was raised by Christina's cousin Constantine Niarchos, the heir to another famous shipping line, who asked Christina for a dance. Pleading exhaustion, Christina declined the invitation. Quick as a flash, Constantine replied, "Oh, come on Christina, it won't cost you $50 million."

Roussel heard the slur and understood full well that it was directed at him. He leapt from his seat and threw himself at Niarchos and the two tumbled over chairs and fell to the floor, grappling with each other as they rolled over and over. Some women screamed, other friends quickly intervened and dragged the two young men apart. Thierry was very angry, more so later, when the dance floor fracas and the reason for it quickly became public knowledge throughout the social circle of St. Moritz.

That fracas, even though initiated by him, was exactly what Thierry didn't want to happen, because now everyone in St. Moritz who knew and cared for Christina watched him, everyone was suspicious of his motives and everyone came to believe that he was not only milking Christina of vast amounts of her money but also seemed set on running all her business matters. Indeed, some feared Thierry's constant demands and his control over Christina might one day result in him gaining control over the Onassis fortunes.

As a result, stories began to appear in newspapers, many of which seemed to carry the stamp of authenticity. Indeed, most of them were emanating from those close to the Onassis extended family. One such story revealed that in an effort to keep her husband in her bed at night while they vacationed on the French Riviera during one summer, Christina paid him $20,000 for every night he stayed with her.

Athina would also read of the will her mother wrote and re-wrote to ensure that her only darling child, her beloved Athina, would have a fortune waiting for her on her 18th birthday and a ready-made, well-run worldwide business empire awaiting her to join and eventually control when she turned 21.

Throughout the summer of 1988, Roussel had been nagging Christina to change her will, cajoling her, even demanding that she delete from her will most of the inheritance that would go to members of her mother's family and leave more to their daughter Athina. And yet this legal argument was going hand-in-hand with Thierry's demand for a divorce from Christina, who was still obsessively in love with him. Sadly and reluctantly, Christina agreed. In trying to persuade Christina to grant a divorce, however, Thierry was open about his reasons. He wanted finally to marry Gaby with whom he had now fathered two children.

Thierry would plead with Christina that Athina's inheritance would be in safe hands if she gave him control of her fortune and the Onassis empire in the event that she might die early. There is no suggestion that Thierry Roussel had a premonition that Christina might die at a young age or at any time in the near future. He was aware of the remarkable number of pills and sleeping draughts, the uppers and downers, Christina was taking each and every day. But there is no record of

Thierry being worried that Christina had any cause to fear a sudden or early death.

She was only 37 at the time of her death, which was no age for a woman to die in the late 1980s. And yet, throughout that summer Thierry never stopped nagging his wife to alter her will. Of course, if the worst had occurred, which it did, and if the 3-year-old Athina had needed a guardian, which in Thierry she had, as night follows day that would mean Thierry Roussel would have every chance of controlling Athina's fortune and maybe the Onassis empire, which he knew was worth billions of dollars.

Athina would read all these facts before she reached age 18 and she most likely had the intelligence to understand the facts, the meanings and the underlying truths surrounding her mother's fortune and also her father's treatment of the mother she had never really known and struggled to recall. Athina must have found it very difficult, if not at times impossible, to equate the deeds of her father toward her mother with the kindness and tenderness with which he had treated her throughout her young life.

Then, at some point, Athina also read the will her mother left.

Christina's last will and testament was, in fact, her ninth. Some days after making her last will Christina told a dear friend in Buenos Aires that re-writing her will had been the hardest night of her life. Christina wrote the will in her lawyer's office in Geneva. The will, which she wrote in English, ran five pages long in Christina's distinctive neat, upright schoolgirl hand.

Seven beneficiaries would share $6.6 million; Thierry Roussel was to receive a life annuity of $1.42 million provided that the annual income produced from Athina's estate was not less than $4.25 million.

Importantly, Christina wrote that everything else "of any kind and description whatever, real or personal, tangible or intangible" she bequeathed "to my beloved daughter Athina to be hers absolutely." She also added a vital addendum: "Athina's affairs are to be managed prudently and diligently until her 18th birthday by a board of four Greeks and Thierry Roussel. A simple majority vote would decide all issues."

But writing that will had been a desperate, heartbreaking wrench for Christina because in re-arranging her will to placate Thierry and provide a fortune for her daughter, it was necessary for Christina to remove many of the close relatives she had always respected and some of the people she had loved. Out went her uncle George Livanos, her aunt Kaliori, four other relatives as well as long-time business associates of the Onassis empire and old friends. Her decision, at the insistence of the man she loved, devastated her.

It seems extraordinary, an incomprehensible coincidence, that exactly one week after writing that will Christina was dead. That was one of the reasons so many people, including relatives and close friends, other family friends and family lawyers wondered whether Christina's death was accidental or whether there had been some unknown, dark forces at work.

Surely, Athina read all this and began to understand. Now she wanted to try and understand why her mother had led such a life, seemingly unable to enjoy a lasting relationship with any man, unable to hold a man with the power of love, devotion or even friendship. Instead, Athina must have feared the more she read, the more she might come to fear what she would read and learn about her mother. Her natural curiosity and the metaphorical umbilical cord that ties a mother and daughter all their lives were too strong for Athina.

She obviously decided to ignore her fears and read all about her mother because only then would she understand what she was really like, what drove her, saddened her, made her happy and why she behaved the way she had throughout her short life. For Athina, however, reading through the intimate side of her mother's life would become more of a pilgrimage than a joy.

Chapter Six

As Athina read through the biographies of her mother, she must have shaken her head in disbelief, wondering if all she was reading was in fact true or had been exaggerated, fabricated or, in some way or another, distorted in an effort to blacken the family name or denigrate her memory. As she read some of the more outrageous and extraordinary facts of her mother's wanton and lustful life, one could imagine that Athina was taken aback.

She had never thought of her mother as such a person, never for one moment imagining that her mother could have contemplated such sexual self-indulgence, let alone lived such a promiscuous lifestyle. Yet Athina must have been really happy when she read that, as a teenager, her mother had enjoyed all that she now enjoyed, spending as much time as possible with her pony. Christina, too, loved competitive games on horseback, spent hours grooming her pony, loved riding and spent most of her waking hours thinking, talking and reading about ponies. The only difference was that Christina had been brought up in England while Athina had spent nearly all her young life in the quiet of a Swiss village. At age 15, Christina's mother had sent her to a boarding school in Switzerland for a year, where she had learned French and good manners.

Christina was sweet 16 and still at school when she met through her father her very first boyfriend, a young Greek boy, Peter Goulandris, whose family owned four shipping lines with more than 130 vessels and worth in those far-off days $1.5 billion. Athina surely became even more puzzled by her mother's wild life because as a teenager Christina was known as a quiet, polite, demure and deferential young woman and, apparently, her relationship with Peter was wonderfully innocent and sweet with no hint of the outrageous sexuality that would come to dominate her life.

Considering that in her 20s and 30s Christina would bed whomever she fancied, seemingly at the drop of a hat, in her younger days she was somewhat of a prude. She strongly disapproved of her father's close relationship with Maria Callas, not only blaming Maria for breaking up her parents' marriage, but Christina also refused to condone her father's behavior in living with Maria and let him know she disapproved. Even at the mature age of 19, Christina was still a virgin and proud of the fact, whereas young Athina was suspected to have lost her virginity soon after her 17th birthday. Such thoughts brought a smile to Athina's lips, but never for one moment did she believe that she would one day follow in her mother's lustful footsteps.

Athina took careful note of her mother's first real love affair and read and re-read every detail of her affair with a man by the name of Danny Marentette, a man a few years older than Christina whom she fell in love with and wanted to marry. She was even more determined to marry Peter, a reasonably wealthy

man, even when her father ordered her not
to. And while she raged at her father for for-
bidding their relationship, Christina suddenly
found herself pregnant.

The marriage was being planned until
the sudden death of Eugenie Niarchos,
Christina's favorite aunt, who committed suicide with an overdose of sleeping pills.
Christina was mortified and Ari, her mother
Tina and others all took the death as a sign
that Christina should not go ahead with the
wedding. Indeed, Ari was certain that aunt
Eugenie had been murdered. The death
caused great drama, anger and sorrow.
Finally, after great pressure from both her
parents, Christina agreed to call off the
wedding and have her baby aborted.

For the following eight months, Christina
lived a quiet, lonesome life as she and her
family continued to mourn the death of aunt
Eugenie. But she was young and she had
tasted the sweet fruits of sex. And now she
wanted to enjoy her life, live a little and find
a new bedmate. By accident, she stumbled
across a dashing, handsome Argentine polo
player in St. Moritz in 1970, when she was
nearly 20 years old. Luis Basualdo was not
rich and not yet a famous polo player but he

was great fun and, apparently, a great lover. Despite her modest sexual experiences Christina, in fact, seduced Luis and began a wild orgy of sex, making love day and night, but managing to spend a few hours on the ski slopes and on the dance floor of the exclusive King's Club.

Athina concentrated on one particular fact that emerged whenever she read of her mother's sexuality — she liked to be dominated by her lovers. As Nigel Dempster wrote in his biography of Christina, *Heiress*: "Christina had shown, first with Danny Marentette and now with Luis Basualdo that she liked her men to take a strong line with her."

But Luis walked out on Christina, back to his former girlfriend, and she was furious.

Apparently Athina laughed loudly when she read of her mother's next lover, Mick Flick, an heir to the Mercedes-Benz fortune. They became friends, they shared jokes, they had a great time together but Mick never wanted to seduce Christina. He only became sexually excited by blondes and Christina was no blonde. So she decided to change her image, went to the hairdresser's and came back a stunning blonde. Within hours of leaving the hairdresser's they were in bed.

Christina would later tell a girlfriend, "Finally we were going to get it together and he was all over me until the moment he took off my panties. There, staring him in the face was my big black bush. Disaster. It was a flop; the blonde trick hadn't worked."

But Christina wasn't yet finished. The following day she raced off to a beauty clinic and left with a big blond bush for Mick's delight and delectation. When she told him of her great sacrifice, Mick suddenly realized that the problem all along had been that he didn't really fancy Christina. He liked her a lot, but didn't find her sexually attractive. And he told her so. They continued to meet from time to time, at parties and dinners, but they never were intimate.

Having finally come to the conclusion that there was little or no future with Mick Flick, Christina suddenly found herself being seriously attracted to a man almost 30 years older! A divorcé, Joseph Bolker was a relatively well-off, handsome and charming real estate man from Los Angeles who looked and acted rather like a younger edition of her father. Christina was attracted, especially when she discovered that he was also kind and intelligent. Within two hours of a dinner

date in London, they went to bed and spent
the next few days there happily making love.
Christina was hooked, despite the fact that
Bolker had four grown-up daughters, the
oldest the same age as Christina.

Bolker was enjoying his fling with
Christina but within a couple of weeks she
was really in love with the man she had come
to rely on, one reason being that Ari was
busy chasing Jacqueline Kennedy and he
had no time for his only daughter. Christina
now became desperate to marry Joe Bolker
but he refused because he was too old, had
four daughters and had no intention of ever
marrying again. That didn't deter Christina,
who simply refused to take no for an answer.
When he still refused to marry the richest
girl in the world, Christina took an overdose
of sleeping pills. When she recovered, she
vowed to continue overdosing until he
agreed to marry her. Within days, Joe and
Christina were married in Las Vegas and she
had not even told her father. Christina was
just 20 years old.

Athina read all of this and immediately
thought of her own life and of her own love
for handsome Brazilian showjumper Alvaro
Alfonso de Miranda Neto, nicknamed Doda,

who is 12 years her senior. She also wondered whether she would want to marry Doda at such a young age if and when that ever became a possibility.

Aristotle Onassis was on Skorpios celebrating Jackie Kennedy's 42nd birthday in July 1971 when he was told the news of his daughter's marriage. He was stunned and, at first, he didn't believe it. When he discovered the wedding had indeed taken place, he became apoplectic with rage and horror at what his only daughter had done. Ari stormed around the villa, shouting, swearing and yelling at the top of his voice at everyone and everything.

"How could she? How could she be so stupid? The stupid, stupid girl," he yelled at anyone who was listening, though in reality he was simply talking to himself.

Within days, Ari had planned and ordered his underlings to spread nasty gossip about Bolker and he kept up the pressure on Christina, stripping her of the $75 million trust fund she would inherit on her 21st birthday. At the same time, Christina had come to the conclusion that although Bolker was a "nice guy" he wasn't really for her. Athina noted that her mother's marriage came to a civilized, friendly end just days after Bolker had thrown a wonderful 21st birthday party for her at Hollywood's famous Le Bistro restaurant.

Athina probably hoped that if ever any relationships of hers came to an end, she would want them to be concluded in such an understanding and kind way. Not yet 18 when she read of these ups and downs of her mother's roller-coaster love life, Athina realized for the first time in her life that she was not only learning one hell of a lot about her mother but also beginning to understand the mother she had never really known.

Athina must have admired her mother's next move in her topsy-turvy life. Her mother moved as quickly as possible to expunge the memory of her short, sweet marriage by throwing herself headlong into the arms of her former lover Luis Basualdo. She was surprised, however, that on her way to Buenos Aires to see her sexy Luis she had stopped off in Rio de Janiero not only to get herself suntanned and fit on the famous Copacabana beach but also took the opportunity to spend her nights in the arms of another handsome, virile and famous polo player Paolo Fernando Marcondes-Ferraz.

After a few hectic nights and lazy days on

the beach, Christina flew off to meet Luis, one of the great loves of her life. Athina wondered if there was something in her genes and her mother's genes that attracted them to gifted horsemen because it seemed that she, too, felt the same way toward them. Christina always felt that polo players made the greatest and most satisfying lovers and although Athina's beau Doda didn't play polo, he is undeniably a great horseman. It is also true that Athina is an accomplished horsewoman and under Doda's tuition she has improved greatly during the past 12 months.

But during those few days with Luis, which Christina later confessed were spent making love day and night, she also flirted with other handsome Argentine polo players, which amused Luis. He had never seen Christina so flirtatious, openly flouting her sexuality for the benefit of a number of his polo friends. And it made him realize that Christina was no longer under his spell as she had been during their time together in St. Moritz but was now a very modern, sexually independent young woman who wanted all the handsome young men she fancied to be attracted to her.

It was at this stage of her life — age 21 — that Christina really found herself sexually and from that moment on her attitude to sex and her own sexual enjoyment and fulfillment became uppermost, if not paramount, in her life. She didn't want to settle down and she didn't want only one lover at any one time. She had finally discovered that she really enjoyed flirting, as outrageously as possible. She also really came to understand that she had a great capacity for making love as well as a prodigious sexual appetite. Some of her lovers would be taken aback by her neverending demands for more and more sex, enjoying two and three hour-long sex sessions with lovers who appealed to her and who had the stamina necessary for such rigorous and demanding sex.

Christina returned to Rio de Janiero, a city she found sexually alluring, the whole place pumping with adrenaline, the nightclubs imbued with a sexual excitement she found no where else in the world. Christina wasn't sure whether it was the music, the handsome men, the beautiful women, the climate, the Brazilians' open attitude to sex or what. She just found Rio gave her a fantastic feeling of *joie de vivre*.

And in Rio she re-discovered one or two of her former lovers as well as some new, young handsome ones, not all of whom were polo players but, she did note, that all of them were highly competent horsemen.

It was while she was enjoying the delights of Brazil that her darling brother Alexander was killed in the plane crash that devastated her and the entire Onassis family, but particularly their father Ari, who was distraught with grief. Christina was now her father's only child and just 22 years old.

Ironically, it was Ari's insistence in the summer of 1973 that a young bunch of men and women come to Skorpios for a holiday because, although he wanted never to forget his only son, he knew that life had to go on and he needed to have youth around him to help him get over the horrendous accident that had taken away his son. And one of those young people invited to enjoy the sun, the sea, the clean air of the Aegean and a summer of wine and good food was Athina's father-to-be, Thierry Roussel.

To Christina, of course, Thierry was a near-perfect young man: handsome, blond, attractive, French, sophisticated and witty. She made a beeline for him, determined to win him for herself despite the fact that she was warned from the very beginning that he wasn't available because he was heavily involved with a beautiful Swedish girl by the name of Gaby.

Christina was warned that if she persisted in trying to corral Thierry, the affair and the relationship would end in tears and disaster. Christina could not and would not be put off. She had made up her mind and she would do her damnedest to win him over. She always hoped that if her personal charms, her looks, her personality and her capacity for wonderful passionate affairs wasn't sufficient then there was always the possibility they might find her wealth so appealing and so attractive that she would win in the end.

And yet, Christina hated having to rely on her father's fortune to win a man she desired. When targeting a new man, Christina often wished that there was no Onassis fortune behind her because then she would truly know that the man wanted her for herself, not for the family fortune he might one day enjoy, if not inherit. Throughout her 20s, that money problem played havoc with Christina in many of her affairs because she always suspected that the young men she fancied were often fortune hunters whose real target was her family's wealth — not her body, her character, her beauty, her personality or her sexual favors.

Sometimes on meeting strange, handsome young men, Christina would play a game with them, adopting a different identity, pretending she was someone else who just happened to look like Christina Onassis. On occasions the ruse even worked — but not for long. Within the circles Christina mixed, everyone knew her too well and when she left those circles she felt like a stranger and her confidence evaporated so much that she lost the appeal which won her a number of her lovers. As a result, Christina reluctantly came to the conclusion that she had little or no option but to shelve those ideas and simply try to sort the good guys from the bad guys, the ones who were attracted to her for herself and those on the make who only had one eye on her and the other on the family fortune. But it was often quite difficult to make that decision.

However, after the death of her father in March 1975 Christina, still only 24, became a changed woman, imbued with a remarkable confidence that no one had realized she possessed. For a couple of years she had been learning the shipping business at her father's New York offices — Olympic Maritime — but within days of his death Christina had grasped the reins of power and was holding meetings and discussions with those senior employees whose job it was to run the various shipping companies.

In the hours immediately following her father's death and though his death had been anticipated, Christina revealed the passion in her character, firstly by trying to overdose within hours of his death and secondly by cutting her wrist in a bid to kill herself. She simply did not want to face the future knowing that she would never again see her beloved father. On both occasions she was discovered almost in the act of attempting to kill herself and, consequently, was easily saved.

Somehow, Christina found the will to battle on, taking a new perspective. Throughout her life she had always strived to please her father, desperate for him to approve of everything she did. Now, following his death, she would show the world that she was indeed a "chip off the old block," an Onassis through and through who had the same willpower, the same business acumen and the same brains to drive the Onassis empire forward to even greater heights. It was a bold challenge for Christina to take up because she had no training or business experience. She had, indeed, simply lived the life of a spoiled little rich girl.

But the famed Onassis willpower and vigor took over and Christina took command of the situation as though she had been running the business for years. And, as if to refute the legend that pleasure should never be mixed with business, Christina came to the conclusion that she needed not just a man in her life but a husband. By chance, she met an old friend from her teenage years, Alexander Andreadis, the youngest son of professor Stratia Andreadis, a wealthy shipping magnate, who had been a close friend of Ari Onassis. A week after their meeting, Christina more or less proposed marriage. Andreadis accepted and one month later they were married.

Within a matter of a few weeks, however, the marriage was in trouble as Alexander assumed the role of the dominant husband and Christina rebelled at the very idea. As Alexander struggled to bring his wayward bride to heel, Christina went her own way doing what she wanted, when she wanted and asking permission of no one. After six weeks, the headstrong Christina called a press conference to tell the world that she had taken personal control of the Onassis empire and she also announced that the Onassis empire would not be merged with the Andreadis assets. It was Christina's dramatic way of letting the world know the marriage was heading for the rocks. One year after the wedding, Christina filed for divorce claiming "my husband is a motorbike freak, despotic, foul-mouthed, blindly jealous and a womanizer as well as being fanatically self-centered."

Andreadis replied that Christina had "a peculiar and dictatorial character, often calling me a peasant." Not surprisingly, the divorce was granted on the grounds of mutual incompatibility. Christina was once again a free woman.

To the world, Christina announced, "I'm through with marriage and romance. I won't let anything stand in the way of running my business now. That is the one major goal in my life."

Ironically, it was a result of her newfound dedication to her shipping empire that Christina accidentally came across the new man in her life — the Russian shipping official Sergei Kauzov — who Christina was trying to persuade to lease a number of the tankers from the Onassis fleet, then lying idle. Sergei was no typical Christina Adonis. He was a slim man with thinning brown hair, a gold tooth, an eye that didn't move; in all a man that no one could describe as handsome. But to Christina he had a certain *je ne sais quoi* despite the fact that he was a member of the Soviet KGB secret service and he had a wife and a young daughter living in Moscow.

Despite all this baggage, the old Christina swooped as she had done in her earlier romantic years and within 48 hours they were in bed. "In bed he is the best," Christina would proudly tell her girlfriends and to test his metal under duress Christina took him off to Rio for Carnival. Romance, the throb of the calypso music, the hot weather, the sexual frisson of Rio once again worked its magic on Christina and within seven days the Western world's most celebrated and wealthy woman had asked the happily married Sergei Kauzov to marry her.

Christina followed her Russian lover back to Moscow and for a while she lived in his mother's ghastly, tiny, ill-equipped apartment with Sergei while he sorted out his divorce. Christina paved the way, giving his wife a golden handshake — $100,000 — for agreeing to a quickie divorce. Sergei's wife could not have been happier. But Christina was far from happy. She hated every moment of her life in Moscow, except for the sex, which she confided to friends was wonderful. The wedding ceremony in Moscow's number one Palace of Weddings, which took place under the hammer and sickle, was a drab affair. And life in Moscow in the late 1970s — cheerless, cold, lifeless and lonely for the world's most spoiled and privileged heiress — was not conducive to a happy start to their married life. In no time, Christina could take it no longer and she fled to Paris. Her life became even more impossible and complicated when she was confronted with the news that Sergei was a KGB agent. That single fact could have bankrupted the Onassis shipping business because all their contracts were with Western oil companies which, at the height of the Cold War, would have been strongly advised by their various Western governments not to do business with a shipping line with Soviet connections. Christina immediately saw the problem and wanted out. She also saw it as an opportunity to divorce Sergei and return to a more normal lifestyle.

But once again she showed her generosity to her Russian bear of a lover, waiting

months to file divorce papers until both
Sergei and his aging mother were safely out
of the Soviet Union. She also gave him a $3.5
million bulk carrier and a $4 million oil
tanker to start his own shipping business.

In November 1979, with the divorce
papers filed, Christina decided she wanted
to celebrate, spoil herself, forget her boring
marital problems, forget her ghastly drab life
in Moscow and push out the boat, determined to enjoy wild, sybaritic nights of
debauchery. Every night for a full week,
Christina left her home at 10 p.m., collected
a handsome man she barely knew and took
him for a night of hedonistic debauchery to
New York's infamous club, Studio 54.

Later, a happy, exhausted and sexually satisfied Christina would tell her closest girlfriends
of her nights at Studio 54, where she was welcomed with open arms, plied with champagne
and, if she wanted them, soft drugs like
cannabis. Those running the Bacchanalian-
style Studio 54 were only too happy to welcome
one of the world's wealthiest women, especially
when she was young, attractive and brimming
with enthusiasm to enjoy everything offered at
the club, including the freedom to have sex as
often as she wished with whomever she

wished. Christina thrived in the corrupt atmosphere that pervaded the club, something which she had never before experienced.

Indeed, Christina always liked being in command of situations. She had a reputation for being forward with men and would often be the one to initiate sex, suggesting to men she barely knew that perhaps they should go to a room immediately and have sex. It was Christina who initiated sex with Sergei Kauzov, it was Christina who suggested to the Brazilian polo celebrity Paolo Fernando Marcondes-Ferraz within hours of meeting him that they should have sex.

In his biography of Christina, *Heiress*, the diarist and author Nigel Dempster examining her life after the death of her father, wrote, "Christina not only fell in love easily but her passion was usually boundless and brief. She turned away from lovers and husbands, and turned toward others, with a capriciousness that was beginning to worry the Olympic hierarchy as well as her family. Her emotional equilibrium, which continued to be achieved only with difficulty and with drugs, made it impossible for anyone to predict her moods, or what or who would take her fancy next."

That summed up Christina's life at that time.

It was in February 1984, 10 years after having a fling with Thierry Roussel, that they finally married, but only after Thierry had warned her that he would not marry her unless she lost at least 30 pounds. By starving and steaming herself Christina lost the weight and Thierry agreed. Less than a year later Athina was born. But, except for brief spells, Thierry rarely made Christina happy. He bossed her about mercilessly and constantly castigated her for putting on weight, for taking too many pills and for looking fat and ugly. In return, Christina simply loved and adored him and showered him with money and gifts. And after Thierry walked out of the marriage to live with his mistress Gaby, Christina would pay him $100,000 for a night of sex.

It would not end there. As poor Christina lost control of her bloated body and her weight soared, she also lost all respect for herself. Thierry was neither the first nor the last man whom Christina paid for sex. She felt ugly and fat and she convinced herself that the only way she could get enough sex was to pay for it. So she did. And she kept taking the pills.

But Christina did have her beloved Athina, whom she adored above anyone. She showered her with presents and with love and she decided she wanted another baby as a companion for Athina. She promised Thierry $10 million on the safe delivery of another baby but Thierry refused, saying that he was no longer attracted her. So, Christina went back to the drugs that gave her highs and the sleeping pills that gave her rest.

In her early 20s Christina had tried both hashish and cocaine but she did not approve of those types of drugs, which she considered dangerous. Indeed, as queen of Skorpios following the death of her father, Christina banned those drugs from the island and would sometimes order guests to leave if she found them participating in drug-taking. She adopted this attitude to illegal drugs because of a number of friends who had become addicts and, as a result, had ruined their lives. James, Marquess of Blandford was one of Christina's childhood friends and they had always kept in touch, but he became a heroin addict much to the distress of his father.

Christina proved how good a friend she could be by planning to kidnap James as she flew with him in her private jet from London to Paris and have him taken by ambulance to the Chateau Gage, a drug clinic with a sound reputation for treating addicts. Previously, James' father had asked him to attend the clinic but James had flatly refused. Christina simply phoned James, inviting him to a great bash she was throwing in Paris and he was thrilled to be invited.

On the trip over he snorted a few lines and was surprised when he saw an ambulance racing along the tarmac to their jet as it taxied to a halt. He was even more surprised when the aircraft door was opened and four burly ambulance men came on board, man-handled him off the plane and drove off to the clinic. James flew into a rage. When he arrived at the clinic, he managed to climb out the window of his second-story room, climb over a wall, steal a motorbike, borrow $30 from a total stranger, use a credit card for a flight to London and was back home the same day. The ruse had been a failure, Christina had lost a friend but she had shown that she was fully prepared to help to cure anyone from their drug addiction.

For most of her short life, however, Christina herself was happy to achieve her own highs through sexual activity. However, she did become heavily dependent on over-the-counter drugs. At times, Christina became seriously addicted to amphetamines and for the last 12 years of her life Christina resorted to tranquilizers, depressants and barbiturates almost on a daily basis — except when enjoying good sex with someone, an activity that seemed to negate her need for her favorite drugs.

Christina used these drugs as if they were nothing more than cough drops until a couple of years before her death, when she met the elegant Jimmy Douglas who had lived with the Woolworth heiress Barbara Hutton for a few years. After admitting she took six or more barbiturates a day, a shocked Douglas exploded, "They are worse than cocaine, worse than heroin. They make you crazy."

She refused to believe these pills were dangerous despite the knowledge that such pills had led directly to the untimely death of her own mother Tina in 1974. Tina was found dead in her bedroom in the Hotel de Chanaleilles, the Niarchos family mansion in Paris. The cause of death was given as a "heart attack or lung edema" (excessive accumulation of fluid in the tissues). A Niarchos family spokesman said that Tina had a "blood clot in one leg and that death resulted when the clot moved to the heart, obstructing blood circulation."

The French newspapers posed the theory that her death had been caused by an overdose of sleeping pills. The *New York Daily News* printed a story from Bernard Valery, its highly respected Paris correspondent who knew the family for some years, stating that Tina's death was caused by "an overdose of barbiturates and tranquilizers." Whatever the cause of death, Christina knew that her mother had a problem with barbiturates and tranquilizers.

That same year, her father Aristotle was diagnosed as suffering from myasthenia gravis, a degenerative muscular disease aggravated by Ari's lifetime of overindulgence in alcohol and the fact that he never went to bed until late at night. After only a few hours sleep he would rise at dawn seemingly rested and ready for a full day's work. Both these habits Ari had enjoyed throughout most of his life. But now he knew that death was not far off. The following year he died. The deaths of her brother Alexander in 1973, her mother in 1974 and her father in 1975 had a calamitous effect on young Christina and as each member of her close family died she would feel waves of panic racing through her brain.

Christina came to believe that the entire Onassis family was to be wiped out within the space of a few years and she feared for her own life. The idea that the following year, 1976, would be the year of her death petrified her.

At different times of her life those three members of her immediate family had been really close to her. Alexander's death in the air crash had knocked the stuffing out of Christina and seriously depressed her; her mother's death had shocked her because she was convinced that her death was not simply an accident of fate but something worse, and the moment of her father's death mortified her. Indeed, for a while, a panic-stricken Christina lost total control of her mind and spent days in a darkened room hardly eating and frightened to go to sleep in case she never woke again.

When she finally got over the trauma of so many deaths coming so quickly, Christina once again turned to sex as her escape from reality.

To a great extent, a young Greek woman named Elini Syros, just a few years older than Christina, who became her personal maid and constant companion, helped save her sanity. It was following the death of Alexander that

Ari Onassis, for whom Elini had worked as a personal maid in Skorpios and Paris, gave her to his daughter. As tragedy followed tragedy, Christina and Elini grew close to each other until after only a year or so Christina would travel nowhere without Elini at her side.

Only once had Christina left Elini behind and that was when she moved to Moscow to live with Kauzov in his mother's cramped apartment. It showed how attached Christina had become to Elini that before parting in a flood of tears she gave her $200,000 in cash so she would have enough money to take care of herself. To a simple but intelligent Greek maid this was a fortune, particularly in the 1970s. Elini's remarkable character and honesty was revealed when Christina returned from the collapse of her disastrous Russian marriage and asked Elini to join her once again. The first thing Elini did was to hand her mistress the $200,000 — every penny of it. She hadn't spent a dime.

Elini had a near-magical calming effect on Christina, the only person throughout Christina's entire life who could soothe her whenever she descended into one of her frequent rages, shouting, screaming, yelling and swearing usually in a fit of frustration over some minor incident or problem. No one dared even approach Christina when she erupted in one of her famous rages except for the tranquil, imperturbable Elini who always had the ability to assuage even Christina's most violent tantrums.

Indeed, so dependent did Christina become on the faithful Elini that when Christina was not sharing her bed with a man she would always insist on Elini sleeping in the room immediately adjoining her bedroom so that she always knew there was someone she could trust close by. And Elini never complained, never demanded and throughout the years she spent with Christina she never asked for a single day off. Perhaps one of Elini's more bizarre duties was to be dragooned into being Christina's dancing partner on numerous occasions.

Christina loved to dance. She felt that dancing was in her blood, indeed in the blood and the soul of every true Greek man and woman. Christina was renowned for being a wild dancer with almost animal vitality and once she hit the dance floor in any nightclub, at any party, any disco there was simply no stopping her. Like her father, she also enjoyed Greek taverna music and she could not enter such a tavern without spending a couple of hours or more dancing with the locals or anyone who chanced to be there. Whenever Christina danced she seemed to be tireless. She would wear out her lovers, boyfriends, husbands and anyone and everyone who would dance with her including women and, when all of these dropped out through fatigue or exhaustion, poor Elini would be called to take the floor and dance until her mistress called a halt. And yet, quite remarkably, Elini would always be smiling and laughing when she danced with Christina, never seemingly affected by the thought that she was simply obeying an order.

And Athina, too, loves to dance.

As yet, however, Athina is showing no sign of playing the role of a wild, natural dancer to anywhere near the extent to which her mother would throw caution to the wind and happily disregard any pretense to polite behavior or gentle decorum by storming dance floors, discos and tavernas in wonderful spontaneous abandon as she danced in almost a world of her own making. Athina not only enjoys dancing, she has also enjoyed nights in Greek tavernas and she loves the music of Greece. Perhaps it will be a matter of a few years before the genes passed onto her from her mother materialize in a similar passion for dancing.

In many ways, Athina must be happy that she has read of her mother's tortuous life and she is determined that she will not follow the same path that ended in a bath full of water in her suite in the Alvear Palace Hotel in Buenos Aires.

Mystery has always surrounded Christina's death. The night before she died she had phoned her beloved Athina, talking enthusiastically about her forthcoming visit to Argentina. "You will love it here," she had told her 3-year-old. "It's wonderful. We shall buy a huge ranch and you will have your own pony."

Christina was enjoying her return to her favorite city, Buenos Aires. She had decided to settle there, bring up Athina in Argentina and throw herself into the fast living, party atmosphere of the capital's social elite. In Buenos Aires she felt attractive and enjoyed the romantic atmosphere of the place, the handsome men who paid attention to her. She believed this was because as a woman from a Mediterranean background her skin color was very much like that of the

Argentinian people. But Christina still hated her massive thighs, which she herself called "tree trunks."

So, before settling in Argentina where she would live with her darling Athina and the ever-faithful maid Elini, Christina decided she had to pluck up the courage to undergo necessary, painful cosmetic surgery. For weeks after the operation at the exclusive Clinique Valmont in Switzerland, Christina was confined to a wheelchair as the scars healed. She was warned the scars would take months if not years to disappear, but her thighs would look more presentable.

There were other reasons why Christina wanted to live in Argentina. She had finally been told by Thierry Roussel, the man she still loved, that their relationship had run its course. He now refused to have sex with her, even at $100,000 a night, because he told her that she no longer held any sexual attraction for him.

It was this abrupt and devastating piece of information that finally persuaded Christina to flee Europe, forget about Roussel and settle in Argentina, where she knew the men fancied her. From age 18 and throughout her adult life, Christina was driven by the fact that she had to be sexually attractive to men. She desperately needed their love, their bodies and their admiration to give her the self-confidence she had always lacked.

While in Buenos Aires, Christina fell in love once again. For 20 years Christina had been close friends with a woman her own age, Marina Tchomlekdjoglou, and many years before she had met Marina's brother Jorge, a quiet, self-assured man who was born in Greece but lived most of his adult life in Buenos Aires. However, though Jorge had always been attracted to women, he had never married. Ironically, the Tchomlekdjoglou family textile business owed Christina a great debt because she had loaned the family $4 million when they were in financial difficulties. Now the firm was thriving once again.

Christina and Jorge met again as friends, but almost immediately a more romantic relationship, which had never before existed between them, began to develop. Overnight, Christina had a smile back on her face and they became an item, with Christina even going to his office each day and sitting around drinking coffee and waiting patiently for her man.

Jorge made her laugh, something which Roussel had never done. Jorge made her feel wanted and pampered and loved and not just for her body. They liked each other, they enjoyed spending time together chatting and laughing and not spending every moment in bed together. To Christina this relationship was something she had never before experienced and she was loving it.

And each morning and every night Christina was on the phone to Switzerland and to her darling Athina. And after each call Christina would speak to Athina's nanny, checking every detail of her daughter's day, including her diet, her sleeping pattern, the clothes she was wearing and her happiness. She also discussed plans for Athina's birthday some months away.

Christina wanted to make Buenos Aires her city, where the Onassis family could re-establish the roots that her father had laid in the city all those years ago when he was a young man in a hurry. Christina was always respected in Argentina and she enjoyed that respect. She didn't mind whether it was because of her extraordinary wealth or that they liked her sense of fun and enjoyment, which was so akin to the Argentine nature.

With every passing day Christina felt that the "death curse" of Jackie Kennedy was diminishing and she felt more secure about her future.

Early November 1988, Christina and Jorge discussed their plans to marry and Christina asked real estate agents to find her a superb penthouse in Buenos Aires and a country estate not far from the capital. Now her future was secure and she no longer needed Thierry Roussel and told him so. She was taking her darling Athina and settling in Argentina. Christina knew the Onassis empire was in safe and capable hands. She wrote instructions that if anything should happen to her, the Greek managers and directors would run the business and keep the fortune intact until her beloved Athina was old enough to take over the reins of power. It seemed to Roussel that he was losing his little girl and his power over Christina. It also meant that he was losing the possibility of living the life of a very spoiled and rich man.

On the night before her death, Christina was the life and soul of a barbecue party. But this was no frantic, pill-induced, forced euphoria but a much quieter, happier, more placid Christina. Jorge was at her side and she looked happier than ever. Together they went for a walk before Jorge retired to his room at the friend's villa just a few doors from Christina's hotel and she returned to her hotel suite. They arranged to have breakfast together the following morning before taking a swim. Christina could now make such early morning arrangements because for the first time in many years she had no need to take pills to help her sleep.

But at 10 a.m. the next day, Elini discovered Christina lying naked in her bath in just two inches of water. The world and the authorities leapt to the conclusion that Christina had died from an accidental or deliberate drug overdose. The postmortem declared Christina died from an acute pulmonary edema of the lung, which had produced a heart attack — the same given for Christina's mother's death 14 years earlier.

However, there was a vital difference. Tina's pulmonary edema had been caused by a massive dose of barbiturates but there was no suggestion of barbiturates in Christina's body. In fact, more than 40 different medications were discovered in Christina's suite but only the diet prescription drug and an insignificant amount of amphetamines were found in her body. Judge Alberto Piotti's official report stated that drugs did not cause Christina's death. There was also no evidence of either an accidental or deliberate drug overdose. Importantly, Judge Piotti's report stated that the investigators did not know what had caused her death. It seems extraordinary if not impossible that the world's wealthiest young woman, still in the prime of life, could have died in a totally mysterious manner with no clues and no evidence suggesting how she died.

Christina's death has remained a mystery. It is only recently that Athina has learned about the mystery surrounding her mother's death. And there are some of her Greek relatives who hope and pray that Athina never touches such drugs as her mother and grandmother before her because they are convinced that it was the culmination of a vast variety of drugs taken over a period of many years that had a cumulative effect on their bodies — and killed them both.

Chapter Seven

Throughout her life, Athina will always be recognized as the last full member of the Onassis clan. Though she bears the name of both her father and her mother — Onassis-Roussel — she will always carry the responsibility of being an Onassis, one of the world's richest and best-known dynasties.

Having lived a quiet, secluded existence for the first 18 years of her life, cut off from the social whirl of the super rich into which she was born, Athina is about to emerge into the great wide world. From now on Athina will be judged not only by her peers but also by the rich, dynastic women of power — society women, editors of upscale women's magazines and those of a similar age who will want to show her that although she might be the richest girl in the world, she can't cut the cake like they can.

And, perhaps more importantly, Athina will be judged and compared to the other Onassis women who came before her; the world's most-renowned widow, Jackie Kennedy Onassis; one of the world's greatest opera singers, Maria Callas; Artemis Onassis, Ari's older sister who became almost a mother-figure to him, and, of course, Athina's mother, Christina.

It seems that Athina has been most fortunate in having spent all her young life under the guidance of her stepmother, Gaby, with whom she still enjoys a close, good relationship. Perhaps Athina has not yet come to fully understand that the quiet, unassuming, practical, motherly Gaby gave her quite a remarkable start in life following the death of her mother. Gaby happily and readily took Athina into her home, into her family and into her life, giving her as much love and affection as she gave her own children. And that love and sense of security has provided Athina with a stable, loving background and given her the emotional stability that may well help her to live a full and happy life.

The odds of that happening in the early days of Athina's life were low, indeed, because the emotional instability of her mother would not and could not have provided Athina with a stable life. Now, despite the enormous pressures that will emerge to test her very fiber, there is a good possibility that Athina's loving and well-balanced childhood may prove both strong and prescriptive enough to weather the most tumultuous personal problems that could face her.

And, through reading, association and distant family relatives, Athina will come to understand that the Onassis women who came before her were formidable comparisons.

The most famous, of course, was Jackie Kennedy, who shocked the world when the news was announced in October 1968 that she and Aristotle Onassis had married.

Following the assassination of Jack Kennedy, the beautiful Jackie had become the most sought-after woman in the world. But, save for the millions of dollars Aristotle was worth in the late 1960s, he most certainly was not the most sought-after man. Short, overweight, pugnacious, ugly and prone to fits of rage, the society women of New York and Washington, let alone Philadelphia were genuinely at a loss to understand Jackie's decision. And they were certainly not jealous of her catch!

As one well-known New York hostess succinctly put it at the time, "Even with all those dollars, how could she?"

Indeed, the hostess was only saying what most women believed — that Jackie Kennedy had married Ari primarily for his money. However, time would show that Jackie's primary reasons for marrying him was that she came to believe that Ari's millions would physically protect both her and her children from the "nutters" who might want to kill them; that in his grand homes in Paris, the south of France and on his private island of Skorpios, which were all guarded and protected, she and her children would feel safe. And, without a doubt, his wealth was also an important contributing factor. As Jackie would prove, she loved spending money, she adored buying clothes.

This author does not know what Athina thinks of Aristotle Onassis' marriage to Jackie Kennedy, but from what she has read it is likely to be the same as most people who now know

the facts — it was a dreadful failure. She knew
that the first two years were successful and
that Aristotle provided Jackie with the physical as well as the emotional security for which
she craved at that turbulent and testing time of
her life. And for Ari the marriage was a majestic notch on his gun belt, which he seems to
have enjoyed with unbridled sexual passion
for the first few months. During the last three
years of their five-year marriage, however, Ari
and Jackie saw little of each other as she traveled the world spending money and meeting
friends and Ari worked his customary 20
hours a day and began, once again, looking at
other women.

The marriage was doomed and the
inevitable wrangling over a payoff began in
earnest. Understandably, Jackie wanted as
much as she could squeeze out of Ari and he
was determined to keep the Onassis fortune
he had built from nothing to stay in the family. It didn't help the negotiations that Jackie
and the main recipient of the Onassis fortune,
Ari's daughter Christina, had daggers drawn.

When Ari died in 1975 at age 69 the lawsuits
over his fortune took off. On marriage, Jackie
had insisted, and Ari had readily agreed, to
make her a cash payment of $3 million — a

reverse dowry — and in return she gave up all claims to his estate. However, instead of receiving money from the estate, Jackie had persuaded Ari in the early years of their marriage to establish a foundation that would distribute funds to Greek welfare organizations on an annual basis and to which Ari agreed to leave half his fortune in his will. Those with unkind thoughts also believed Jackie suggested the plan to spite Christina.

As well as the $3 million, Ari had also bequeathed Jackie a $250,000 annual tax-free payment, $50,000 of which would go toward the support of her children, Caroline and John. But Ari also insisted that if Jackie contested his will, every effort should be made to fight the case, the costs to be paid from his estate.

It was then that Jackie showed her true colors, contesting the will and demanding a huge payoff. Many believed the real reason was her hatred and jealousy of Christina rather than the actual money. However, that hatred was returned in equal measure by Christina.

From the moment that Ari told his daughter of his involvement with Jackie Kennedy, the young Christina took unkindly to the arrival of such a celebrity in the Onassis family. Following her brother's tragic death, Aristotle had become more closely involved with Christina and she had reveled in the fact that after so many years her father had turned his full attention on her, showering her with gifts and his love. Christina feared that once again her father would turn away from her and instead shower attention, gifts and love on his new wife.

Within a few months of Ari marrying Jackie Kennedy, young Christina became consumed by enmity and jealously toward her stepmother. And then she read a magazine article suggesting that Jackie Kennedy might be bedeviled by a death curse.

Christina once told Kiki Feroudi Moutsatsos, her father's personal secretary: "I have always known that Jackie was a curse. Before she entered our family we were strong and well. Now the Kouris brothers are dead, my aunt Eugenie is dead, my brother is dead. Olympic Airways (part of the Onassis business empire) is slipping away and so is my father. Before she came to us, she was by her American husband's side when he died. My unlucky father had to go and find her and bring her to our shores. Now the curse is part of our family and before long she will kill us all."

From the moment Christina came to that

conclusion, there was no changing her mind until Jackie Kennedy also died. Indeed, when Christina visited her sickened father she would tell him of her fears of Jackie's death curse. At first, Ari would hear none of Christina's nonsense, telling her not to be so silly but, only some months before his death, Ari came to believe in Jackie's death curse and he stopped upbraiding his daughter for her fearsome contention.

And that was the reason why Christina, following the death of her father, was prepared to do anything in her power to remove Jackie from having any connection, no matter how tenuous, with the Onassis family and the Onassis empire. Following Ari's death, lawsuits followed, as Jackie sought to extricate as much as possible from the business empire. Her persistence paid off and, as a result, Jackie became a wealthy woman. Firstly, Christina offered Jackie an $8 million payoff, which she instantly spurned. Finally, in a bid to bring the lawsuits to a conclusion and get rid of the hated Jackie, Christina offered a remarkable $20 million. Jackie grabbed it with both hands.

In return, Christina insisted on an end to all lawsuits, the promise that Jackie would never again visit Skorpios and that she would give up all rights to Ari's fabulous yacht, the *Christina*. Christina felt vindicated and victorious because in her mind she had finally rid the Onassis family of the death curse that she so feared.

Now that Athina has reached the age of 18 she has come to learn more about the maternal side of her family. During her early years, Athina learned more about her father's and her stepmother's family histories but very little about the Onassis dynasty. Indeed, she knew very little about her maternal grandmother whose name she had hardly ever heard spoken.

In her early teens, Athina set about learning all she could about the Onassis family by reading biographies. And she started educating herself by reading of her grandfather's early life.

Aristotle had remained a bachelor until age 43, enjoying many affairs but working seven days a week and many long nights in his determination to build one of the world's great shipping lines. As the world knows, he succeeded brilliantly. A high-school dropout, Aristotle Onassis had arrived in Argentina in the early 1920s as an emigrant — alone, desperate and poverty-stricken. To earn a living, he became a streetseller, pushing trinkets on street corners, and a shoeshine boy for the dandies of Buenos

Aires, earning just a few pesos a day. This was a tough time to be a nobody in a country like Argentina and the situation would become worse as the world economies nose-dived and the Great Depression sucked the lifeblood out of those with nothing to their name.

But Ari's luck turned in 1925, when he was accepted as a trainee electrician with the British-owned United River Plate Telephone Company. The pay was at poverty level but there was a bonus; the exchange he worked in employed 200 young Argentine girls on the switchboards. Ari was no Greek Adonis but he had charisma, personality and a warm smile, which endeared him to the girls even though he was rather short and not exactly handsome. He was built like a young ox with powerful shoulders and, as his daughter Christina came to regret to her eternal annoyance, large, powerful thighs. And now it seems the young, athletic Athina may have been blessed with the same curse. She is only 18 years old, but already she hates her thighs and her butt which are beginning to resemble those of her late mother.

Later, Ari would recall with a great smile on his face, his work at the exchange, "I had to work in overalls squatting on the floor behind the switchboards and every time I looked up there was row after row of women's legs." He quickly learned Spanish and the girls found this young, well-built Greek attractive. But Ari had more important matters on his mind than women.

He volunteered to work as a telephone operator on the night shift and began listening to the calls coming from London and New York. He listened with growing interest as he realized many of the calls were between wealthy clients and their stockbrokers. He began to play the stock market and earned himself $1,000 within a few weeks. At that time, $1,000 U.S. dollars in Argentina was a small fortune, especially for someone with nothing.

With this lucky break he bought himself a couple of smart suits, shirts, ties and shoes and joined an exclusive rowing club on the Tigre river. With his easy style and European manners he was soon accepted by the younger members, especially some of the young, middle-class girls. But Ari needed quick money so that he could play the role of a young, wealthy European socialite enjoying Argentina. He branched out into new moneymaking areas — running a string of young prostitutes, selling bootleg whisky and peddling dope!

Buenos Aires was a hive of activity in the late

1920s, the richest, most powerful and aggressive state in South America. Rich in most areas, Argentina lacked a good tobacco industry. Ari saw his opportunity, imported some excellent Greek tobacco with the help of his father Socrates and made $500 on his first deal. That was the foundation of his shipping empire.

It was because of his dramatic success in selling Greek tobacco that the Greek government appointed him Greece's deputy consul in Buenos Aires, a major coup for the ambitious young man. The appointment propelled Ari into the Argentinian society in which he wanted to move; mixing with the wealthy, the powerful and the beautiful. But his name began to appear in U.S. Army intelligence reports passed to J. Edgar Hoover in Washington, D.C. They showed this young Greek was working for the Greek Intelligence Service and, as a perk, was permitted to obtain large sums of Western currency at the official rate of exchange and sell it on the black market, garnering him thousands of U.S. dollars. Within three years he had amassed an amazing $1 million.

With that money he purchased six laid-up ships from the Canadian National Steamship Company for the ridiculously cheap price of

$125,000. It was the depths of the Great Depression but Ari's luck was riding high. He met and so amused a Norwegian divorcée named Ingeborg Dedichen, whose father just happened to be one of Norway's foremost ship owners, that she fell in love with him. Ari used this contact to order three oil tankers from Sweden. The outbreak of World War II found Ari's three brand-new oil tankers in enemy hands.

Ari spent most of World War II in the United States and it was in New York that he met the young teenage Greek girl, Athina Livanos, whose father was another famous Greek ship owner. Athina, whom everyone called Tina, was just 14, Ari was a portly, rather middle-aged 43, but only admitted to being 37. Unbelievably, Ari claimed later that he fell in love with Athina the moment he met her. She was the precise opposite of Ari and he loved her for that. She had been well brought up in an exclusive part of London, educated in an English boarding school for young ladies and spoke impeccable English with an upper-class accent.

At the end of World War II Ari was considered an unsuitable man for any young well-educated girl, known as a womanizer with a dubious past, a gambler and a drug dealer who had somehow acquired money by dubious means. Indeed, if the Livanos family had known of Ari's plan to marry their daughter they would have slapped her in a convent, because Ari was determined to take Tina's virginity and then persuade the Livanos family to let him marry her to avoid a scandal.

Ari seduced the 16-year-old Tina on his launch in Oyster Bay in April 1943. He was gambling that Tina's father would not charge him with statutory rape for fear of a scandal; and by taking her virginity, Ari had ruined Tina's chances of marrying anyone else. It took three years for Tina to persuade her parents to let her marry the paunchy middle-aged Ari. A year later, another Greek shipping tycoon, Stavros Niarchos, married Tina's elder sister Eugenie and became Ari's archrival.

Like the young Athina Roussel, her grandfather Ari Onassis was also brought up hardly knowing his own mother. She died when he was 12 years old and he was brought up by his older sister Artemis to whom Ari had a close life-long relationship. His devotion to Artemis was revealed to anyone permitted to enter his large cabin on the *Christina* because on the wall behind his bed was a large portrait of Artemis.

An energetic, intelligent woman with a powerful personality and a commanding presence, yet she weighed only 95 pounds. And throughout Ari's life she looked after him like a mother, yet she was only two years older. She would fuss over what food her brother ate and, remarkably for such an independent man, this continued throughout his life.

Even as a 50-year-old billionaire, Artemis would still watch what he ate whenever she was present. She was the only person permitted to make such comments as "My darling, don't take too much spicy sauce it might make you ill" and even reminding him not to eat too much food because it might make him fat. He took it all without a murmur of complaint.

And yet there was also a love-hate relationship because in most other matters he would not accept advice or interference from Artemis. It was only in maternal matters, like his diet, his weight or his health where Artemis was permitted to go so far as to tell him what to do, what to eat or what not to eat. In other matters, he would turn on her, telling her to mind her own business, get out of his life and stop telling him what to do. In her turn, Artemis was physically afraid of him as she knew other woman were at various times throughout his life.

The faithful Ingeborg discovered Ari's cruel side all too frequently during their six years together. When Ari drank too much and, for no apparent reason became belligerent and argumentative, he would take it out on poor Ingeborg. Sometimes he would turn vicious and violent, knocking her about and sometimes felling her with a flurry of punches and then kicking her while she lay on the floor pleading for mercy. And he never apologized afterward, remarking not only to Ingeborg but also other lovers he beat up, "Every Greek beats his wife; it's good for them; it keeps them in line."

Though Ari quite frequently berated Artemis for whatever reason, he never let a day pass without phoning her, no matter on which continent he was at the time. She was like his lifeline and he needed her to be there, just like a young lad wants his mother to be around in case he needs her.

But Artemis also had the nerve and the courage to confront Ari if she believed he was making a mistake, even about his love life. Artemis took a distinct dislike to the famous Greek opera singer Maria Callas with whom

Ari enjoyed an on-off passionate relationship over many years. Artemis looked down on Maria, telling Ari she would not be suitable on two counts — she was from Greek peasant stock and she was overweight and fat. When Ari told his sister he was seriously thinking of marrying Maria she would berate him, telling him not to be "so silly" because such a marriage would only end in disaster.

Artemis would tell him, "You don't like fat women; you like slim women like Tina and Jackie Onassis, not fat women." And she would taunt him saying, "Within a month, you would not want to make love to her anymore and that would lead to another marital disaster."

She would encourage him to look else-where, saying, "You have plenty of money; women love money, especially beautiful women because they want to spend, spend, spend to keep themselves beautiful, always wanting expensive dresses, shoes, coats, everything. There are many more beautiful women for you out there, waiting for an affair with the world's wealthiest man. Don't waste your time on a fat Greek singer."

And, with those comments, Artemis knew that she was on safe ground because Ari loved beautiful women, adored making love to beautiful women just as much as he loved making lots of money. As a boy he learned French, perfect French, because he was taught privately by a beautiful young French woman with whom he fell in love. Later, he would tell how she would give him French lessons while they made love and when resting afterward she would make him decline French verbs. Ari became a fluent French speaker with a good Parisian accent.

To Aristotle, however, it mattered not a bit what his sister thought about one of the great loves of his life, Maria Callas, with whom he enjoyed a passionate love affair with all the elements of a Greek tragedy.

Ari's secretary for many years, Kiki Feroudi Moutsatsos followed the dramatic adulterous love affair between the two greatest living Greeks from close quarters. The world knew that Maria Callas was the world's greatest prima donna and that Ari Onassis was one of the world's wealthiest men and yet they only wanted to live a very private life together. Kiki would write in her book *The Onassis Women*, "From the moment they became lovers, the *Christina* (yacht) was the place where both of them felt the most comfortable together."

As Artemis explained to Kiki, "Maria feels

protected there. There are no crowds begging for her autograph or photographers pursuing her with their cameras and no fans asking when she will perform next. She is safe there. My brother makes sure of that. Besides, she is a very private person and it suits her to be only with him ... Maria also believed her own husband, Meneghini, mistreated her, using her terribly and making a fortune off her talent. My brother would never do that to her. He is taking care of her now. The rest of us she does not need. Only him."

Some Greek opera lovers believe that Maria gave up her wonderful career for Aristotle, though this is disputed by others who believe that by the time they met, the greatest years of Maria's exhausting career and the effect it had on her voice were coming to an end. Ari had fallen in love with Maria when she sang *Medea* at London's Covent Garden, having pursued her for months. Their love affair began when she accepted an invitation for a three-week cruise on the *Christina* in 1959, along with Sir Winston Churchill and his wife. At the end of that cruise, Maria told her husband that she had fallen in love with Aristotle.

But Ari changed Maria's life forever and she admitted so. There were some opera lovers who believe that after Maria fell in love with Ari her voice took on a new, richer, depth of expression.

Artemis would say later, "Maria's opera career came to an end because as a perfectionist she came to the conclusion that she could no longer perform to the high standards she set herself. And Ari offered Maria a new life that she had never before contemplated."

Kiki would write, "Ari took all the passion that she poured into her voice and provided another outlet for such energy and ardor: him. Instead of standing on the stages of the great opera houses of the world, facing an impassioned and demanding audience, Maria now stood beneath the cypresses of Skorpios and faced only one adoring fan. While he did not offer her 16 curtain calls and tumultuous applause, he redirected the sensuality she had previously poured into her music. She was no longer merely a diva; now she was a woman. The sun and the ocean and the flowers and the trees at Skorpios replaced the lights of the stage and, like a flower that had been denied the light of the sun, she suddenly blossomed into a luscious, exotic rose."

But there were many highs and lows in their affair.

Toward the end of the 1950s it seemed that Maria and Ari would marry. In November 1959 Maria divorced her husband Meneghini, a man whom she believed had used and abused her, forcing her to carry out nonstop performances around the world purely for financial gain. Meneghini was Maria's agent and manager as well as her husband. She never forgave him.

Within days of Maria's divorce, Tina finally divorced Aristotle on the grounds of adultery after 12 years of marriage. For nine years, Maria and Ari were an item, spending as much time together as was possible. In many respects they were an ideal couple; Ari, confident, strident and demanding; Maria, quiet, shy and introspective. Despite Maria's dearest wish to marry Aristotle and have children with him, for some unknown reason, he never asked her to marry him.

Those that saw Maria and Ari together spoke of them as the perfect couple who enjoyed relaxing in each other's company and who would happily spend days and weeks together either sailing on the *Christina* or spending days lazing on sunny Skorpios. Both enjoyed each other's company and both wanted privacy for just the two of them.

Some believe it was the influence of Artemis who persuaded Ari that marriage to Maria would not be sensible. She would tell Ari, "You and Maria will never be happy together because you are both too much alike. You are both big bosses. If you marry you will end up killing each other."

Understandably, Maria was angry and distraught when Ari suddenly turned around and married Jackie Kennedy because even if they had not married, Maria wanted to have Ari's child to complete her life. Once, she did become pregnant by him but miscarried. That single emotional event caused Maria serious depression.

Ari's secretary, Kiki Feroudi Moutsatsos would write, "There was little doubt that Jackie's success in winning Mr. Onassis' love and name broke Maria's heart. Many of us worried about how she would survive such a shock. But we soon learned that marriage did not mean their love affair was over. One month after his marriage to Jackie, Mr. Onassis was in Paris seeing Maria. If anything, their love appeared to grow stronger."

But friends say it was the relationship between her mother Christina and her grandfather, Aristotle Onassis, that Athina Onassis

Roussel wanted to investigate and understand above every other relationship within the Onassis dynasty.

From reading biographies, Athina learned that the defining nature of her mother's entire life was the single fact that she was the daughter of Aristotle Onassis. For Christina, being a child of Ari Onassis was an insurmountable burden that she was never able to shake off throughout her short life. It caused her unhappiness and misery because she never felt a free spirit, never felt she was an individual in her own right but always that she was the child of Ari Onassis.

Kiki would write of her, "Even when her only child Athina was born she could not savor that moment because fear of her daughter's safety had already begun to plague her. Although there were certainly many times, especially when she was a teenager, when Christina appeared carefree and full of life, her leaden veil of misery was poised and ready to cover her face at a moment's notice."

Life was never kind to Christina. And many who have studied Christina's relationship with her father, a relationship that totally dominated her entire life, knew the reason. She wanted one gift more than any other but she was never given it: her father's love. She felt that her older brother Alexander was the child that Ari really loved and that in his love for his only son he was unable to give the same time, the same love or the same commitment to her, his only daughter. Kiki would note, "Just one moment with the three of them — Ari, Alexander and Christina — and anyone could see which of the two children the father preferred." It was a burden that Christina found impossible to carry without wilting and feeling sad and unloved.

After reading that account of her mother's life, Athina must have understood for the first time the real reason for the trauma of her mother's life; the reason that she was so shy and unhappy, the reason for her pain and anguish which so many people had commented on. Athina probably understood immediately what her mother endured throughout her life as she strove to please her father, to win his love and to grab his attention.

Erik Christopher Francois Landhage had been born only a few months after Athina in 1985, but Thierry Roussel did not tell his wife Christina that a baby boy had been born to Gaby and that he was the father. It was 18 months after Athina was born that Christina first discovered that Gaby and Thierry had a little boy. Understandably, she was absolutely furious, enraged with Thierry who was still her husband. Suddenly she understood why Thierry was always working somewhere overseas on one new project or another and mostly at her expense.

That discovery left Christina feeling numb, cold and unloved. Christina came to suspect that Thierry might have been using the millions of dollars she had given him to enjoy an enhanced lifestyle with Gaby and their son rather than on the business ventures that nearly always seemed to fail and sometimes fail spectacularly. It seemed to Christina that Thierry was simply using her, pretending to pay court, pretending to love her, occasionally making love to her — all so that he could get his hands on her money to enjoy a better life with his mistress.

Those thoughts made her deeply depressed and wondering what was so awful about her that made the man she loved walk away from her for weeks at a time. But because she was so depressed Christina made matters worse by standing naked in front of the mirror, revealing to herself that she was so ugly and so fat no man would ever again want to spend time with her or make love to her. She would try to convince herself that it was her fault Thierry didn't want to spend time with her because she had let herself go, let herself get fat and all because she lacked the determination and strength of character to diet properly, to exercise enough or to stop eating the food she knew she shouldn't.

Athina must have recalled that she had first met her stepmother Gaby when her mother Christina was still alive and she had sensed at the time that they were simply good friends who vacationed together. It was only in her teens that Athina came to know that her mother had made the extraordinary decision to become friends with Gaby so that the three could co-exist together sharing Thierry, the man both women loved. Perhaps Athina recalled that her mother would send gifts to young Erik and she read later that, on occasions, she even loaned Thierry her private plane to fly to Malmo in Sweden to see Gaby and baby Erik.

It was only during the past year that Athina learned that her mother had drawn up an agreement with Thierry. He would spend the bulk of his time with her at her home in Switzerland while he would spend seven days a month with Gaby and Erik in Malmo.

However, any time he spent away on business would not affect the seven days a month he spent in Malmo. From the date of that agreement it seems that Thierry began spending more and more time away, flying around the world in Christina's private jet putting together business deals. Sometimes Gaby would accompany him. Most of these business deals would eventually end in failure and it seems that Christina was left to pick up the tab, which would sometimes run into tens of millions of dollars.

In June 1987, Gaby and Thierry had another baby, a girl they named Sandrine. Three months later Thierry summoned the courage to tell Christina the news himself and she was mortified. At first, she flew into a rage, followed by oceans of tears. "I am like an Arab woman, sharing my husband with a concubine."

Christina vowed to be rid of Thierry once and for all and yet she was still deeply in love with him, perhaps more than any other man she had ever known. She couldn't understand how Thierry could want another family when he already had one, a wife who loved and adored and spoiled him and baby Athina who adored her father. But this latest betrayal finally convinced Christina that she could not keep any dignity if she permitted the marriage to continue. She feared that when the news leaked out that Thierry Roussel had produced yet another baby with his mistress while still married to Christina she would become a laughingstock. Her pride couldn't take that. She had suffered enough. So in September 1987 she secretly filed for divorce in the tiny mountain village of Celerina near St. Moritz.

And then a more bizarre twist took place.

Christina simply could not start a new life, finding new lovers. She still had her darling Athina but she knew she needed a man in her life and the only man she wanted was Thierry. So, a remarkable dinner took place for 12 people in a Geneva restaurant during that autumn to which Gaby and Thierry were invited along with nine other people who were good friends of Christina's. All were informed of the unique reason for this dinner — the first meeting between Christina and Gaby, the two mothers of Thierry's babies.

Only a single man sat between Christina and Gaby and, as the dinner progressed the two women began to talk. Three hours later they left the restaurant and the start of a firm friendship had been sealed. Within a few weeks Gaby and her children began to visit Boislande, Christina's lakeshore estate, where she had created a child's enchanted dream world with playgrounds, a walk-in zoo, a miniature 4x4 Land Rover, an indoor swimming pool for children and rooms full of toys.

And what Christina quickly came to see and love was that her darling Athina had found two friends with whom she could happily play. And Christina was happy that Erik and Sandrine were happy, charming, blond, blue-eyed children who got on so well with her own dark-eyed, dark-haired Athina. Within weeks Christina began lavishing gifts on Erik and Sandrine whenever they came to visit, which the children loved. As a teenager reading these facts of her early life, Athina would strive to recall the events. Sometimes she did remember instances but at other times she could not do so.

However, reading these affairs of her childhood probably made Athina realize that her mother must in many ways have been a remarkable woman, someone who didn't fall in and out of love at the drop of a hat but always wanted a complete, happy, loving and fulfilling relationship with only one man.

Athina hoped that she, too, would meet a man with whom she could enjoy the same relationship. Her mother's topsy-turvy love life forewarned her that she had to take the greatest care before throwing herself into the arms of any man.

Chapter Eight

Despite the fact that Athina has been brought up in Switzerland, attended Swiss schools, enjoyed friendships with Swiss boys and girls, lived in a small Swiss village, speaks French, English, Italian and Swedish fluently but has never been taught any Greek, she is still very much a young Greek woman. Athina not only looks like the epitome of a refined young Greek girl reaching maturity but she also has much of the character and personality of her mother.

She is also a good-looking, statuesque young woman who always commands attention when mixing with a group of teenagers or 20-some-things. She has the flashing eyes and the flashing smile of a young Mediterranean woman enhanced by beautiful dark hair and a wonderful pale olive complexion. She can look stunning with a presence that some people find disturbing in someone who is still so young.

Athina is older than her years. She is intelligent, bright and quick-witted though she can sometimes be quiet, cool and brooding. When discussing matters of a serious nature with a group of young people, Athina has the ability to argue convincingly and intelligently and to make her case almost like a lawyer addressing an issue.

Importantly, she seems to have discovered that she can enjoy herself immensely without worrying what other people think. She also loves to dance without feeling embarrassed. In this respect Athina follows in her mother's footsteps and she now dances for hours on end wearing out any who dare to partner her.

People remark that there is a passion about her dancing, a sense of abandonment and real emotion that excites those who watch her. And it is when she is dancing in such an intoxicated fashion that people remark how beautiful she looks, her eyes flashing brilliantly, her movements almost balletic and spiritual. And her smile can be devastating.

As her stepmother Gaby told friends, "Athina has the power to slay men. She has a wonderful, engaging smile."

It is when Athina lets herself go, her inhibitions forgotten, that she seems to have inherited her mother's proud Greek legacy and out of earshot of the Roussel household Athina says she is proud to be her mother's daughter, mindful of the responsibility she carries of being the last Onassis.

And that responsibility has already reared its ugly head. While Athina was happily growing up in a loving household in Switzerland, unknown to her, legal battles were raging among lawyers in courts across Europe. The lawyers representing her Greek ancestry and those battling on behalf of her father Thierry Roussel have locked horns in court on numerous occasions during Athina's young life.

When Athina was barely 10 years old, the trustees of the Onassis billions, the men responsible for protecting her fortune and ensuring the Onassis wealth increased, were hearing reports that Athina was not growing up in the traditional Greek way and they were of the belief that as an Onassis that was an important part of her development. The trustees asked why Athina was never taught Greek though she speaks four other languages — French, English, Italian and Swedish.

Her father knew that one day Athina would inherit the fortune and the responsibility of running the huge money-spinning Onassis empire, which has always been staffed and run by men and women who speak the Greek language. To them, with Athina's destiny bound up in a Greek company, why would he not arrange for her to learn the language of her birth?

Another example put forward by the Graybeards, as Thierry Roussel calls her Greek guardians, was that Athina was putting blond streaks in her black, thick hair something they had never seen girls in Greece practice, even for fun. And the Graybeards saw photographs of her at age 11 dressed exclusively like a rich little Swiss girl with no suggestion of her Greek background.

The lawyers had asked Roussel to permit Athina to spend some time each year in Greece, or perhaps on Skorpios, so that she kept in touch with her Greek background, but he turned down the request. This worried the Graybeards, who feared that Athina was being kept from her Greek ancestry so that when she became an adult she would feel no empathy toward Greece or recognize no identity with the Greek nation.

The Graybeards — the four Athens-based lawyers — worried even more when it appeared that Athina was being used to promote her father's own pet charity — Action for Childhood — a charity that he started and funded with money given to him and his wife to care and protect Athina. The Graybeards feared that Thierry Roussel was using Athina and a little of her fortune to promote the charity and using her in the publicity shots published in European magazines.

Athina was pictured with the other three Roussel children, Erik, Sandrine and Johanna sitting with their father in the drawing room of a villa and watching a film clip of him carrying out humanitarian work. The Graybeards believed that the primary reason Action for Childhood was receiving the attention it did was solely because Athina Onassis was seen to be involved in the charity. And the world knew that meant there was a real possibility that some of her extraordinary fortune might be used to push that particular charity — bringing Thierry fame and, maybe, fortune.

However, one of the directors of France's most prestigious magazine, *Paris-Match*, maintained that Thierry Roussel had made it a condition of publication of the story about his newfound charity that the Onassis name was never to be included in the text — only Roussel. Twice a year *Paris-Match* paid good money for exclusive pictures of the Roussel family, including, of course, Athina. And the text emphasized how hard Thierry worked for the charity and the underprivileged children.

Thierry argued that his interest in such a worthwhile charity was based on his ability as an entrepreneur as well as his keen interest in international child relief. He expected that, in time, Action for Childhood would finally bring him the world-renowned recognition of his abilities for which he still yearned.

Thierry Roussel, however, has a problem that has dogged him most of his adult life. He has always wanted to succeed in life as an entrepreneur, a gifted achiever, a businessman and a man of action, but yet the history of his business activities suggests that he has achieved very little success in any of his entrepreneurial exploits. And, because he is a proud man, that hurts.

Marrying Athina's mother proved an extraordinarily lucrative move by Thierry. They had first met in her teens, but their relationship really took off when she met Thierry's father, Henri, at a party at London's Claridge's some years later. He was a distinguished part of Paris society in the 1970s, a man of wealth and reputation. Henri Roussel's family founded France's largest pharmaceutical company. Henri sold his share of the company to his brother, lived the life of a rich entrepreneur and made a fortune for himself in Spanish real estate. His son wanted to emulate his illustrious, charming and successful father.

Intelligent, well-educated, extroverted and handsome, Thierry attracted great attention from all the women who crossed his path. He was a most eligible bachelor. In his bid to make his fortune and his mark in life, Thierry pursued a variety of business ventures ranging from publishing and advertising to modeling and home furnishings. Most, however, ended up losing money.

After their marriage, Thierry took the opportunity to prove what a great entrepreneur he really was. Backed by Christina's money, Thierry wanted to join the world's elite, showing that he was one of them, an entrepreneur par excellence. From the start of their marriage Christina began transferring rather handsome chunks of her fortune to her handsome husband. Those running the various parts of the Onassis empire became worried that more and more of the hard-earned Greek assets were being handed over to her husband, a Frenchman, for what they saw was no particular reason. By some calculations Thierry had been handed $50 million within the first few years of their marriage. Indeed, before her death it was understood that Christina had handed Thierry $73 million.

Those Greek businessmen overseeing the Onassis company became even more alarmed when Thierry demanded a major say in how Christina's many financial interests and businesses should be run. They only had Thierry's record of failed business ventures with which to judge him and that did not look promising. Indeed, to some employed in the Onassis empire, Thierry's wish to become involved in the decision-making appeared positively dangerous.

It was perhaps not surprising that the

Graybeards placed Athina's father more in the context of a gold digger than an entrepreneur. They have noted that throughout the years of wrangling over the Onassis fortune, Thierry devotes a great deal of time to this battle. For his part Thierry has claimed that he can prove how much success he has achieved in business. But this is dismissed by the Athens lawyers.

Stylianos Papadimitriou, the lawyer who became close to Aristotle and who heads the Onassis Foundation, says Roussel has bordered on bankruptcy three times in his life. He claims that Roussel spends an astonishing $12 million a year looking after and protecting Athina. That money, of course, belongs to Athina, not her father.

The legal arguments between Thierry Roussel and the Greek lawyers began shortly after the Onassis fortune left by her mother was passed to her daughter Athina, who was nearly 4 years old. That initial row ended with the Onassis Foundation confiscating Christina's Falcon jet. Later, the lawyers demanded that Thierry account for the $12 million he spent each year protecting Athina.

In turn, Thierry, who had been given a place on the management board in his capacity as Athina's father, attempted to gain control of his daughter's fortune. The Greek lawyers were stunned and alarmed at this move and determined to never let the Frenchman gain control of the Onassis fortune.

As the lawyers continued their defense of the Onassis billions and tried to cut back on the amount of money Thierry Roussel claimed necessary to protect his daughter, they were suddenly faced with a new and extraordinary charge. Thierry accused the Onassis establishment of hiring Israeli agents to kidnap Athina and take her to Greece. It appears there was no foundation whatsoever to the kidnapping charge but the lawyers were worried because it appeared to reveal an increasingly desperate attempt by Athina's father to take control not only of his daughter but also of her fortune.

To those closely involved with the trials and tribulations of the young Athina, which have swirled around her as she grew from a child to an independent teenager, it does seem extraordinary that Thierry Roussel should want to cut off his daughter from her Greek ancestry. It has to be accepted that not only during the lifetime of Athina's mother but also since her untimely death, Thierry has personally become a very wealthy man as a result of receiving tens of millions of dollars as gifts or as recompense for duties performed on behalf of the Onassis family and his daughter.

Yet, it would appear from his actions that Thierry believes that what he has received has not been sufficient recompense for his endeavors or his involvement with Christina and Athina. It also appears extraordinary that he should not want Athina to have anything whatsoever to do with her Greek ancestry and background when he knows that she is due to inherit a fortune from her mother's estate.

To many, it seems extraordinary that Thierry, an intelligent man, should run the risk of being accused of pure greed in his pursuit of his claim to have the power of authority of his daughter's wealth, which had been entrusted to faithful lawyers of the Onassis family, handed over to him. His track record as an entrepreneur and businessman leaves much to be desired and there would appear to be no reason why on earth he should seek such power unless his desire for greater wealth knows no bounds.

Still, as the court actions reverberated around innocent Athina, Thierry Roussel did once give permission for her to visit Skorpios, the Aegean island that her grandfather Aristotle bought and developed into his own personal little piece of paradise. It was on Skorpios that Aristotle would relax and enjoy himself, entertain his friends and relations, his children and their friends as well as his wives. On Skorpios Aristotle had enjoyed his own little kingdom and many who visited the island commented on the peace and quiet and tranquility of the place in the blue of the Aegean.

Only once throughout Athina's childhood was the golden girl of Greece permitted to visit the native land of her ancestors. In the summer of 1994, when Athina was only 9 years old, her father took Athina and his other three children to visit Skorpios. Together they walked around the little island, inspecting everything, running hither and yon, racing through the villa her grandfather built as well as some of the other properties on the island.

Despite the fact that no direct descendant of Aristotle has visited the island since Christina's death in 1988, the entire place had been kept immaculately. After her sudden and unexpected death the Athens lawyers decided to retain some 50 members of staff who had worked on Skorpios for years to look after the island, the olive and cypress trees and the various properties Aristotle had built after he purchased the piece of rock and scrub. Their duties hadn't changed one bit since Christina had last visited the island in the months before her death. It was as though the staff expected her to make a reappearance at any time.

Aristotle had spent a fortune converting the island into a private village with various-sized houses and the beautiful villa he had built for himself. The lawyers decided to keep the place and retain staff to look after the property for fear of trespassers or sight-seers, in case Athina might want to live there or simply keep it as a holiday retreat when she was old enough to make that decision.

Indeed, this visit by Athina was the first time she had ever been permitted to meet any Greek people and, understandably, the women working on Skorpios wanted to make a fuss of the little Onassis girl who would one day be their boss. They welcomed Athina and because some spoke English they were able to chat with her though not fluently. Athina must have been taken aback by the attention and fuss, but the little girl smiled her way through the reception, shaking hands with some of the staff but no traditional, warm Greek cheek-kissing took place. Understandably, the meeting was a little forced but the women chatted away among themselves as they tried to decide which member of the Onassis family Athina resembled.

The four children played on the sundrenched beach, swam in the warm blue waters of the Aegean and took out the powerful Jet Ski for spins around the island. Athina piloted the fast, powerful Jet Ski while her father sat behind her. During a 15-minute run, the 9-year-old Athina really gunned the machine, skimming at speed over the water while Thierry hung on grimly.

Watched by the Onassis employees, a determined-looking Athina wasn't laughing or shouting as she piloted her father around and around the bay but had a look of serious concentration on her face. She was simply showing off to her father and those watching on the island and she enjoyed her competence at handling the Jet Ski at such high speeds. When she returned to shore, her brother Erik and sisters Sandrine and Johanna begged Athina to take them for spins on the Jet Ski. It was obvious to those watching that this was not the first time Athina had ridden such a vehicle because she was surprisingly competent for one so young.

But the watching Greek employees noted much to their disappointment and chagrin that Athina spoke only in French to her father, her brother and sisters and never once addressed any of the employees in Greek. She could barely speak a word of Greek and for a member of the famed Onassis family not to speak Greek was like a Frenchman not being able to speak French.

It was also on this visit to Skorpios that Roussel gave one of his rare interviews, describing the philosophy of his relationship with Athina, saying, "My role (as Athina's father) is essentially to prepare Athina to be herself, even if that isn't what people are expecting. My greatest pride would be for her to be well-adjusted like my other children, that she feels part of the family. She calls my wife Mummy and speaks to her in Swedish, like her brother and sisters. She is entitled to a carefree childhood. I don't want her to be treated like a wise monkey. I don't want her to become a cult figure. I don't want her to be treated differently from other children."

Athina's father had taken extraordinary precautions for this visit. Fearing that something might happen to his precious charge, Thierry had sent SAS-trained guards ahead to scour the island, check the fishermen who patrolled the sea surrounding the island and to make sure that all the men and women living on the island were legitimate employees. Throughout the days they remained on the island, armed guards kept watch 24 hours a day, patrolling the coastal waters and warding off boats that came too close for comfort.

But the older women who had prepared many a meal for Christina contrived to gently seduce the young Athina by cooking her delicate Greek meals, which they felt certain she and the other children would enjoy. And they did, they loved the food the women cooked, especially the honey-sweet desserts they produced, much to the joy of the cooks. The women felt this was perhaps the one way in which they could entice Athina to return and bring her siblings with her. To these employees the very fact that Athina is the last Onassis makes it even more important to them that she spends time among Greek people, time on Skorpios and time enjoying her life as a happy, passionate young Greek woman and not as simply another wealthy Swiss miss from western Europe.

Athina had enjoyed her few days on Skorpios watching the women, all dressed in traditional, long, black shapeless dresses, collect the olives and bake them into bread, pick the fruit from the trees and make sure everything was in perfect order because this was the first time in eight years that they had a full member of the Onassis family actually visit them. Of course, we can guess that Athina also visited the island farm, fed the animals and watched as the fishermen returned to port and unloaded the day's catch. It was new and exciting to a little girl whose home in Lussy-sur-Morges is no ordinary villa with lovely gardens but almost a small fortress with a guard room, high electrified fencing, heavy-duty motorized gates, barracks for the guards and round-the-clock security by armed guards. Indeed, Thierry Roussel had taken expert advice to ensure that his beloved daughter was as safe as possible from any kidnappers or intruders.

On Skorpios all was so very different. Here, Athina was free to roam and rush about as she wished, swim in the sea and walk all over the island without fear or restriction. Understandably, she loved the freedom.

But her father had treated the visit to Skorpios like a military operation, planning every move, directing his troops guarding the place, setting up lines of fire against possible armed attackers as well as installing a mobile communications center in one of the rooms of the villa where they were staying. It seemed all too much for the peasant Greek women who wondered why Athina's father should go to such lengths when the only people within sight were those who loved Athina and every Onassis who had spent time on the island. As one Greek woman put it, "She is the last person in the world we would harm. Indeed, we would protect her by every means available if unwelcome visitors came calling. She would always be safe here."

And, of course, Skorpios was the holiday home where he had been persuaded by Aristotle Onassis himself to court his beloved Christina and, maybe, even earn a place for himself in the hierarchy of the Onassis business empire. It had been Aristotle who had seen how Christina had reacted to Thierry, following him everywhere with her eyes, flirting with him and behaving like a young girl who was falling more in love with him at the passing of each day and each evening.

And Thierry recalled how he had been seduced by the peace and tranquility of the island, the warm, starlit nights, the moon on the waters surrounding the island and the times he and Christina had walked along the beach together, a young couple happy with the world and in love with one another.

And it was on Skorpios that Thierry Roussel came to understand the deep connection felt by all members of the Onassis family to their beloved Greece, their native land of which they were so proud to be a member. And he wondered whether his little Athina would one day feel the same pride and passion for Greece or whether her upbringing and education in Switzerland among primarily French-speaking people might have had such an effect on her young mind that her love for her mother's homeland would never be as strong as it was to her mother.

At the end of the holiday Thierry Roussel confessed, "Skorpios is very beautiful but it is also emotionally charged. Several times, Athina has picked some wildflowers to put on '*Maman* Christina's' grave on the island although I don't think she remembers her mother."

To Athina, the holiday on Skorpios was probably more about playing with her siblings than thinking about the mother she could barely remember. And yet the Greek women who looked after her and fussed around her talked in their broken English to Athina, telling her of her lovely mother who had been taken from them at such a young age. The holiday must have been an emotional experience for Athina because she always considered Gaby to be her mother despite the fact she knew that she wasn't.

Sometimes, when growing up, Athina called Gaby "*Maman*," but as she got older she has taken to calling her simply "Gaby" as though she had come to realize that her mother had died. Perhaps seeing her grave in the patch of land reserved for the Onassis family had a greater impact on her young mind than was first realized.

Athina is not someone who chats aimlessly about everything and nothing all day long. Generally, Athina is a quiet, self-contained girl who always gives the impression that there is a lot going on in her brain which she prefers to keep to herself rather than sharing her emotions. Sometimes, she would be as boisterous and bubbly as any other child, chattering away excitedly, but most of the time she seemed happy to let the world pass her by and yet keep an eye on everything that was going on around her, yet keeping her thoughts to herself.

During her years of puberty, Athina was naturally prone to tantrums, bad moods, sulkiness, irascible behavior, quick to take offense and easily piqued. But not all of the time.

All that soon passed, however, and her beloved ponies were a wonderful source of interest. She showered them with affection, petting and grooming them constantly, fussing over them and spending many of her free hours around the stables. In the process, however, Athina has become a first-class horsewoman and there is every possibility that in the not-too-distant future she might even set her eyes on taking part in national and European events. In the distance the Olympic games is also on her agenda and, fortunately for Athina, she has the money to buy the very best horses in the world. In the higher echelons of eventing and show-jumping, money can be the difference between success and failure.

On Jan. 29, 2003, Athina gained not only her independence as an adult but she also officially gained control of her amazing $3 billion fortune. Of course the Athenian lawyers will still control the Onassis empire on her behalf because she has no training whatsoever that would equip her to run such a vast and complicated empire. So far she has received little more than pocket money because her father had no wish to totally spoil his little girl.

To what extent Athina becomes involved in the business remains to be seen. Firstly, she has to talk to the lawyers, who will explain everything to her. Throughout her life Athina has come to recognize that her father has looked after her affairs and has not fully understood the problems that have arisen between Roussel and the lawyers. Thus far in her young life, Athina has, understandably, been guided by her father and she has not known of the charges and counter-charges flying between Thierry Roussel and the Onassis lawyers.

Now, of course, Athina will soon have to learn for herself but she will need to be educated and trained to understand the complexities of the business and of the various and varied financial complications and investments that have been made in her name during the past 15 years.

It may be that Athina wants to attend

university somewhere, perhaps in the United States or somewhere in Europe, to complete her education at the highest level. And, of course, she has plenty of time to do so. But that is looking increasingly unlikely.

According to the terms of her mother's will, Athina does not have to take over the reins of power or, indeed, even get involved in any way with the business until she reaches age 21.

In the meantime, Athina has more important work on her hands — preparing and training herself and her horse for the Athens Olympic games. She is enjoying all the hard work, the tough coaching lessons and the discipline required to reach the very top. And she has her handsome, hunky Doda to love and for company, advice, fun and sex.

But Athina seems to believes that her youth is for enjoyment and she has expressed no intention of embroiling herself in the problems or the decision-making of the Onassis Foundations, the worldwide business empire or the complexities of investment managing. She has her annual allowance as well as one of the largest fortunes in the world and, at this time, Athina probably prefers to leave well alone those who have tended the Onassis legacy for some years and she appears to have confidence that they can continue to do so for some years to come.

Maybe later, some years later, she may become involved. What does the future hold for the richest girl in the world? Only time will tell.